PETERBOROUGH
TO
LINCOLN

Vic Mitchell and Keith Smith

MP Middleton Press

Front cover: Passing Sleaford North Box on 7th December 2013 is class 7P 4-6-2 no. 70013 Oliver Cromwell *with the "Lyndum Fayre". More details of the site are in caption 63. (J.Whitehouse)*

Back cover: 1947 Railway Clearing House map.

An early train on the Cranwell Branch, devoid of details. (Unknown)

Published May 2016

ISBN 978 1 908174 89 5

© Middleton Press, 2016

Design Deborah Esher
Typesetting Cassandra Morgan

Published by
       Middleton Press
       Easebourne Lane
       Midhurst
       West Sussex
       GU29 9AZ
Tel: 01730 813169
Email: info@middletonpress.co.uk
www.middletonpress.co.uk

Printed in the United Kingdom by Henry Ling Limited, at the Dorset Press, Dorchester, DT1 1HD

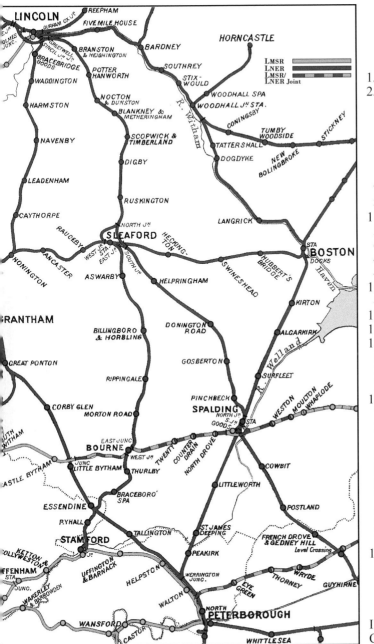

CONTENTS

INDEX

I.   1947 Railway
Clearing House map.

ACKNOWLEDGEMENTS

We are very grateful for the assistance received from many of those mentioned in the credits, also from M.Back, J.Bonsall, Dr. B.W.L.Brooksbank, A.J.Castledine, G.Croughton, M.Dart, G.Gartside, F.Hornby, J.Horne, S.C.Jenkins, D.K.Jones, N.Langridge, B.Lewis, J.P.McCrickard, A.C.Mott, R.Owen, Mr D. and Dr. S.Salter, N.Sprinks, T.Walsh and in particular our always supportive families. Our gratitude also goes to M.Greenwood of the Leicester Transport Heritage Trust. The RAF Cranwell College pictures are reproduced with the kind permission of the Commandant and the help of T.Pearce, Librarian.

GEOGRAPHICAL SETTING

Peterborough was on the northern fringe of Northamptonshire, in the Soke of Peterborough. One mile after our first stop, we pass over the River Welland and the remainder of our journey is in Lincolnshire. As far as Sleaford, we travel over the level ground of Parts of Holland and then enter Parts of Kesteven. Dutch engineers had brought their skills for the reclaiming work on The Fens, from tidal mudflats to productive farm land. Much of the network of drains was made navigable and was ideal for the initial movement of root crops, for onward conveyance by rail.

From Sleaford north to Lincoln, we run along the eastern foot of a ridge, which links the Cotswold Hills with the North Yorkshire Moors. Its varied geology includes red sandstone and limestone. Our route south from Lincoln via Navenby is along the western foot of the hills, where outcrops of ironstone generated much rail traffic, north of Honington.

The area of the Navenby line was drained by the River Brant, which flows north into the River Witham. This runs through the historic City of Lincoln. Through it runs the Witham Navigation, which was purchased by the Great Northern Railway in 1846.

The maps are to the scale of 25ins to 1 mile, with north at the top, unless otherwise stated.

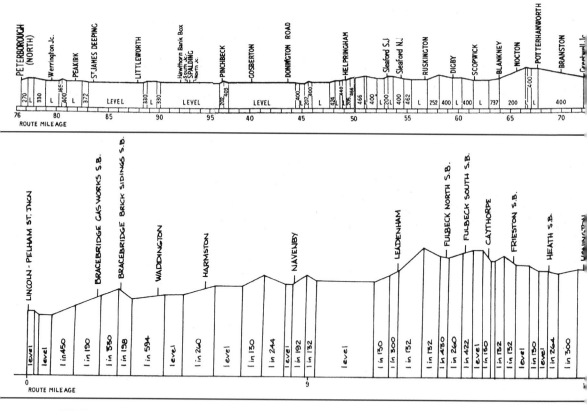

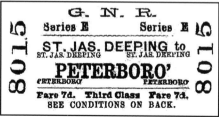

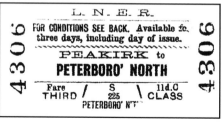

HISTORICAL BACKGROUND

Our route north to Spalding received its Act on 20th June 1846 and was opened by the Great Northern Railway on 17th October 1848. Other lines arrived in Peterborough thus: the London & Birmingham Railway from Northampton in 1845, the Midland Railway from Stamford in 1846, also the Eastern Counties Railway from March in 1846, the GNR from Huntingdon in 1850, also from Grantham in 1852, and finally the Peterborough, Wisbeach and Sutton Bridge Railway, which arrived from the east in 1866. Its spelling of Wisbeach was changed later and it became an MR/GNR Joint Line in 1893.

Our study moves northwards to Spalding, where we find the GNR's 1848 line continues to Boston northwards and its 1867 route from March appears from the southeast. The Norwich & Spalding Railway opened from the east (from Holbeach) in 1858 and the Midland and Eastern Railway came from the west (from Bourne) in 1866. Both were M&GN Joint from 1893.

Our journey north was possible from 6th March 1882 to Sleaford and on to Lincoln from 1st August 1882, the route being a GN&GE joint operation. The east-west line was created by the Boston, Sleaford & Midland Counties Railway in 1857-59, the GNR taking control in 1865. The GNR arrived from the south (Bourne) in 1872. The passenger service ceased in 1930 and local freight in 1956.

Lincoln received its first trains over the MR from Nottingham in 1846. The GNR arrived from Boston in 1848, the year in which the Manchester, Sheffield & Lincolnshire Railway opened from the north. This became the Great Central Railway in 1897. It ran west to Retford and beyond in 1850. The GNR operated north to Gainsborough from 1849, this becoming GN&GE Joint in 1879. The line from Lincoln south to Honington opened on 15th April 1867. The final route opened in 1896 and ran west through Tuxford, under the control of the Lancashire, Derbyshire & East Coast Railway. This became part of the GCR in 1907.

The grouping of 1923 brought the GER, GCR and the GNR into the London & North Eastern Railway. The MR and the London & North Western Railway became constituents of the London Midland & Scottish Railway. Upon nationalisation in 1948, its Eastern Region was formed mainly by the LNER, while most of the LMSR became its London Midland Region.

Closures of passenger stations, goods yards and adjacent routes are detailed in the captions. The Navenby line closed almost completely in 1965, it having lost its passenger service on 10th September 1962, except at Leadenham.

Privatisation of the main line resulted in Central Trains running services from 2nd March 1997. The franchise was moved to East Midlands Trains on 11th November 2007.

Still known as "The Joint Line", the route from Peterborough to Lincoln and on to Doncaster was subject to a major upgrade in 2012-14. This was mainly to increase capacity, so that the increasing freight traffic could be diverted off the high-speed main line.

PASSENGER SERVICES

The tables below give an indication of the number of trains running each way on at least five days per week. Their origin and destination are shown in some of the timetable extracts and the captions.

Peterborough to Spalding					Spalding to Lincoln					Navenby Route		
	Stopping		Fast			Stopping		Fast				
	Weekdays	Sundays	Weekdays	Sundays		Weekdays	Sundays	Weekdays	Sundays		Weekdays	Sundays
1873	6	1	2	1	1883	4	0	4	1	1869	3	1
1895	6	1	2	1	1899	5	0	4	1	1892	7	1
1925	7	1	3	0	1920	4	0	2	1	1922	6	0
1942	5	0	2	2	1940	2	0	2	0	1944	7	0
1960	4	0	6	2	1960	3	0	3	3	1961	6	0
2015	13	0	0	0	2015	8	0	0	0			

Until 1939, most trains on the Navenby line called at all stations, but soon thereafter it was limited to three and just one in final years. All trains ran to and from Grantham. Please see the timetable near picture 115 for the final service.

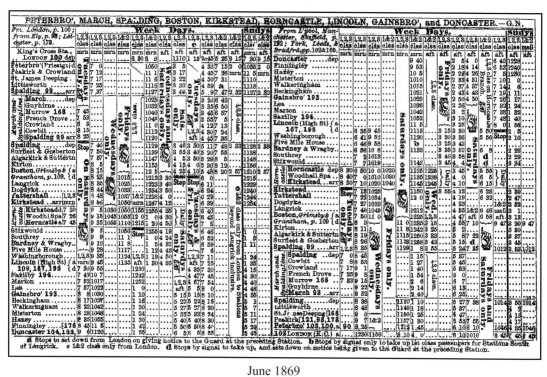

PETERBRO', MARCH, SPALDING, BOSTON, KIRKSTEAD, HORNCASTLE, LINCOLN, GAINSBRO', and DONCASTER.—G.N.

June 1869

June 1883

MARCH, SPALDING, SLEAFORD, LINCOLN, and DONCASTER.—G. N. and G. E. Joint. [Sn

June 1920

MARCH, LINCOLN, GAINSBORO', DONCASTER, and YORK.—G. N. & G. E. Joint.

Miles from March.	Down.	Week Days mrn	mrn	mrn (Fridays only.)	mrn	mrn	mrn	non	aft	aft	aft	Sundays mrn	non
	Liverpool Street, 245 London .... dep.				5 53	10 5		12 0		2 35	4 50	9 55	
	245 CAMBRIDGE 242. "				8 20	1145		1 31		4 12	6 13	1124	
	242 YARMOUTH (Vaux.) "					1016				3 8	4 0	7H 0	
	242 CROMER (G.E.).. "					9 15				2 22	3 33		
	242 NORWICH (Th.).. "				6 19	1120				3 58	5 5	7G19	
	233 HARWICH (Town) "					1010				12J8		8 35	
	241 IPSWICH .... "					1058				12J30	2 18	9 25	
—	March .... dep.		6 55		1015	1 12		3 25		6 50	8 30	1216	
3½	Guyhirne		7 2		1021			3 32			8 37		
6¼	Murrow 273, 273a		7 8		1027			3 38			8 43		
9	French Drove		7 13		1032			3 44			8 49		
12¼	Postland §		7 19		1038			3 50			8 56		
16¼	Cowbit		7 25		1044			3 57			9 3		
19½	Spalding 273, 273a, 298 arr.		7 31		1051	1 37		4 6		7 15	9 9	1241	
	dep.		7 34		1053	1 39		4 10		7 18	9 15	1247	
21½	Pinchbeck		7 39		1058			4 15			9 20		
24½	Gosberton		7 44		11 3			4 20			9 25		
28	Donington Road		7 51		1111			4 27			9 32		
33½	Helpringham		8 0		1120			4 36			9 42		
38½	Sleaford 298a, 298b, 299 arr.		8 8		1129	2 3		4 44		7 42	9 51	1 13	
	dep.		8 16		1132	2 5		4 48		7 46	9 54	1 15	
43½	Ruskington		8 24		1140			4 56			10 3		
46	Digby .... [land		8 30	1055	1146			5 1			10 8		
48	Scopwick and Timber-		8 35	11 0	1151			5 6					
50½	Blankney *		8 40	11 5	1156			5 11		8 3	1016		
52	Nocton and Dunston		8 45	1110	12 2			5 16			1021		
54	Potterhanworth .... [525		8 50	1115	12 7			5 21			h		
56½	Branston †. [483a, 516,		8 55	1120	1212			5 26			1029		
59½	Lincoln (H.St.) 298, arr.		9 5	1130	1221	2 35		5 36		8 22	1039	1 47	
102¼	516 SHEFFIELD (V.).. arr.		1050		2 10	5 5		8 9				4 8	
143¼	517 MANCHESTR (L.R.) "		1242		3 50	6 53		1011					
149½	517 " (Cen.) "		1219			7e23		9 48				5 36	
—	276 London (K.C.)... dep.		4 55		8 45		1130		1 45	4 0	6 5		12 0
—	Lincoln (High St.)... dep.	6 55	9 50		1245	2 41	4 18	5 41	7 24	8 40	1043	1 55	4 19
66	Saxilby	7 6	10 1		1255		4 29	5 51	7 34		1053		4 30
70½	Stow Park	7 14	10 9		1 3		4 37	5 59	7 42				4 38
73½	Lea	7 20	1015		1 9		4 42	6 5	7 48				4 43
75½	Gainsborough ‖ 511, 516 arr.	7 25	1020		1 14	3 1	4 48	6 10	7 53	9 2	11 6	2 16	4 49
	dep.	7 27	1023		1 16	3 3	4 50	6 12	7 56	9 5	11 7	2 17	4 50
78½	Beckingham	7 33	1029		1 22		4 56	6 18	8 2				4 56
80	Walkeringham	7 38	1034		1 27		5 1	6 23	8 7				5 0
81	Misterton	7 43	1038		1 31		5 5	6 27	8 11		1117		5 4
83	Haxey and Epworth 623	7 49	1044		1 36		5 10	6 32	8 16			2 30	5 9
86½	Park Drain	7 55	1050		1 42		5 16	6 38					5 15
89½	Finningley	8 2	1057		1 49		5 23	6 45	8 24				5 22
96½	Doncaster 277, 510, 517, 561 arr.	8 14	1110		2 0	3 30	5 35	6 56	8 40	9 32	1139	2 48	5 33
	dep.	8 55	12 0			3 57	6 10	7 58	9 22	9 37	12 7	3 4	9 22
115	Selby 566 .... arr.	9 21	1237			4 22	6 51	8 23		10 0		3 29	9 49
128½	York ¶ 534, 558a.. "	9 48	1 12			4 50	7 24	8 49	10 5	10 25	1251	3 54	1020

NOTES.

- e Except Saturdays.
- G Via Stowmarket and Cambridge.
- H Yarmouth (South Town), via Ipswich, Bury, & Cambridge.
- h Stops at Potterhanworth to set down from London.
- J Via Witham, Dunmow, and Bishop's Stortford.
- * Blankney and Metheringham.
- † Branston and Heighington.
- § Station for Crowland (4 miles).
- ‖ Over 1 mile to G. C. Station.
- ¶ 1¼ miles to York (Layerthorpe) Station, Derwent Valley

January 1944

Table 64 GRANTHAM and LINCOLN

Miles	Week Days only	mrn	mrn (Via Sleaford Tables 54 and 61)	mrn	mrn	aft	aft	aft G	aft F
	1 London (K.C.).... dep	4 15	..	7 23	10 10	1 25	4 0	5R50	5R50
—	Grantham .... dep	7 40	9 55	11 38	12 53	4 4	6 42	8 33	8 39
4½	Barkston	..	..	..	..	..	..	..	..
6¾	Honington	7 51	10 9	11 49	..	4 15	6 53	8S44	..
9¾	Caythorpe	7 58	..	..	..	4 22	7 0	..	..
12¾	Leadenham	8 3	..	12 0	1 13	4 27	7 5	8 55	8 59
16	Navenby	8 9	..	..	..	4 33	7 11	..	..
19	Harmston	8 15	..	..	..	4 39	7 17	..	..
20¾	Waddington	8 19	..	..	..	4 43	7 19	9 8	9 12
24¾	Lincoln .... arr	8 27	1117	12 20	1 31	4 51	7 27	9 16	9 20

Miles	Week Days only	mrn	mrn (Via Sleaford Tables 61 and 54)	mrn	mrn	aft	aft	aft
	Lincoln .... dep	7 0	7 45	9 12	1035	2 23	4 28	6 25
4	Waddington	7 8	..	..	1043	2 31	..	6 33
5¾	Harmston	7 12	..	..	Aa	..	..	6 37
8¾	Navenby	7 16	..	..	1053	..	..	6 43
12¼	Leadenham	7 23	..	9 31	11 0	2 44	4 47	6 50
15	Caythorpe	7 29	..	..	11 6	..	..	6 56
18¼	Honington	7 35	9 6	9 41	1112	..	4 57	7 2
20¼	Barkston	..	..	..	..	..	..	..
24¾	Grantham .... arr	7 46	9 18	9 52	1123	3 6	5 8	7 13
130	1 London (K.C.).... arr	1054	..	12R30	1 50	6Y2	8 0	9 55

Aa Calls when required. F Fridays only. G Except Fridays.
R Restaurant Car between King's Cross and Grantham. S Saturdays only.
Y Arr. King's Cross 5 53 aft. on Saturdays.

November 2008

Peterborough → Sleaford, Lincoln and Doncaster

Miles			EM	NT	EM A	EM	EM	NT B	EM	NT B	EM	NT B	EM	NT B	EM	EM	NT B	EM	NT B	EM C	NT B
—	London Kings Cross 15	⊖ d					06 35				07 30		08 40			09 35		10 35		11 35	
0	Peterborough 3	d	06 30				07 32				08 40		09 35			10 43		11 50		12 41	
16½	Spalding	d	06a57				07a58				09 02		09 58			11 05		12 12		13 03	
35½	Sleaford	a									09 30		10 26			11 33		12 40		13 31	
—		d			06 55	07 45			08 46		09 31		10 27			11 33		12 45		13 32	
40	Ruskington	d			07 02	07 52			08 53		09 38		10 34			11 41		12 53		13 39	
47¼	Metheringham	d			07 12	08 02			09 03		09 48		10 44			11 51		13 02		13 49	
56¾	Lincoln	a			07 26	08 17			09 16		10 02		10 58			12 06		13 16		14 02	
—		d		07 04				08 27	09 18	09 27		10 27		11 27	11 55		12 27	13 18	13 27		14 27
62¾	Saxilby	d		07 14				08 36	09 27	09 36		10 36		11 36	12 04		12 36	13 28	13 36		14 36
72¼	Gainsborough Lea Road	d		07a26				08 49	09 40	09 49		10 49		11 49	12 17		12 49	13 40	13 49		14 49
93½	Doncaster 7	a						10 36	10 09	11 36		12 35		13 36	12 47		14 36	14 17	15 36		16 36

		EM	NT B	NT E	EM	NT	EM	EM	NT	EM	EM	EM	NT	NT	EM G	EM	NT
London Kings Cross 15	⊖ d	12 30			14 10		15 30	16 35				17 30				19 33	
Peterborough 8	d	13 48			15 09		16 25	17 32				18 35				20 28	
Spalding	d	14 10			15 32		16 47	18a01				19a02				20a54	
Sleaford	a	14 38			16 00		17 15										
	d	14 40			16 10		17 16			17 55	19 01				20 11		
Ruskington	d	14 47			16 18		17 23			18 03	19 08				20 18		
Metheringham	d	14 57			16 28		17 33			18 13	19 18				20 28		
Lincoln	a	15 11			16 45		17 48			18 26	19 31				20 41		
	d		15 27	16 27		17 22			18 24	18 29	19 33		19 43	20 27			21 27
Saxilby	d		15 36	16 36		17 31			18 33	18 41	19 42		19 52	20 36			21 36
Gainsborough Lea Road	d		15 49	16 49		17a43			18a45	18 57	19 54		20a04	20a48			21a48
Doncaster 7	a		17 36	18 35						19 26	20 24						

E To Hull (Table 29)
G To Nottingham (Table 27)

A To Leicester (Table 53)
B To Adwick (Table 29)
C To Newark North Gate (Table 27)

1. Peterborough to Lincoln

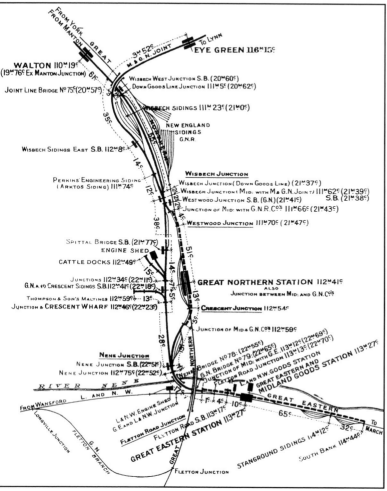

PETERBOROUGH

II. The MR's 1912 diagram has our starting point just below centre; the GN station was termed "North" from 1st July 1923 until 6th June 1966. Below is the GER station, which had the suffix "East" between the same dates; it closed on the latter date. The line westwards was in use from 1845 to 1972 and later became part of the Nene Valley Railway, a preserved line. We travel north on the route marked FROM YORK.

1. This postcard view is from the early 1920s and it has the roof seen in picture 3 on the left. On the right is the porte-cochére over the main entrance and the tower beyond it is over the stairs at the end of the footbridge. Residents numbered 6959 in 1841, this rising to 63,780 in 1961 and 184,400 in 2011. It was Britain's fastest growing city. (P.Laming coll.)

III. The 1925 survey at 6ins to 1 mile has North Station near the lower border and the line to Kings Lynn curving over the others at the top. Lower right is part of the historic city, which has a partly Norman cathedral. The Guildhall dates from 1671.

2.   Passing North Box on 23rd September 1948 is class A2 4-6-2 no. 60520 *Owen Tudor*, a type introduced in 1943. It is working from Leeds to Kings Cross. The city had developed a wide range of products, from baking equipment to laundry machinery. (G.Coltas coll.)

3.   The 4.10pm from Boston on 26th August 1950 was hauled by no. 69808, a class A5 4-6-2T. The MR had its own station west of these platforms in 1858-66 and it was called "Crescent". Its trains ran into "East" thereafter. That station had been built by the ECR. (R.M.Casserley)

4.   Departing from platform 6 on 16th August 1958 is the 3.00pm to Grimsby, which would call at all stations to Louth via Spalding. In the distance are the bow-string girders of the 1913 Crescent Bridge. It replaced a level crossing, which had caused great delays to road users. (P.H.Groom/ M.J.Stretton)

5.   A view north in 1960 has platform 2 on the right, this being used by trains destined for London. Platform 1 was a bay at the north end of No.2. There were three staff crossings over which parcels and mail bags were carried in large quantities. Access to platforms 5 & 6 was through the gap in the wall on the left. (J.Langford)

6. The through platform numbered 6 is seen more clearly in this picture from the same era. It was opened on 1st August 1866 for MR trains. Class 9F 2-10-0 no. 92036 heads a train of empty wagons. Following renumbering, on 28th December 2013, a new platform 3 serving the ECML up fast through line plus an additional down island (platforms 6/7) on the west side, serving the March lines only, were brought into use. Also on this date, the short up bay platform 1 at the south end was abolished and platforms 2 and 3 were both extended and renumbered 1 and 2 respectively. (R.S.Carpenter)

7. The tracks, platforms and signalling were all altered in 1968-69. Through running was speeded up (from 20 to 115mph) with the provision of two tracks devoid of platforms. We look north on 15th March 1990 as a DMU rests between duties to Spalding. The main building and the eastern part of the footbridge were replaced in 1976-80. This bridge was created with slopes to accommodate mail bag trolleys. (M.J.Stretton)

8.   The revised layout is seen in two photographs taken on 21st July 2015, following changes made during 2014. The upgrades mainly related to passenger facilities. The platforms on the right became 4 and 5. Beyond them are 6 and 7, which were completed in December 2013, together with a through freight line beyond. Nos 6 and 7 were used by March trains. (V.Mitchell)

9.   On the same day, we see no. 66759 closer plus the straight and uncluttered tracks northwards. The final route closure in the area came on 4th October 1970 when the line to Spalding and Boston was closed, although Peterborough to Spalding was reopened on 7th June 1971, with a shuttle service of three trains each way per day. This service was improved in 1982 following closure of the March to Spalding section of the former Great Northern & Great Eastern Joint Railway, when the Lincoln to Cambridge service became Lincoln to Peterborough. (V.Mitchell)

10.   New England engine shed can be seen near the top of map III. It was first under GNR ownership and was photographed on 20th May 1938. Featured is no. 025, an M&GN engine. Its tender is fitted with a mechanical tablet apparatus. The shed was coded 35A from February 1950 and 34E from January 1958 until January 1965, when it closed. Opposite was the ex-MR Spital Bridge shed, which was 31F when closed in 1960. (H.C.Casserley)

11.   Here is the new diesel depot on 26th May 1969. It had an inspection pit and fuelling facilities. Nearest is no. D276. The locality had once been famous for the production of electrical appliances, fruit canning and corsets, plus many other specialities. (R.S.Carpenter)

12.   We move on to 29th May 1994 and enjoy the environs as a Driving Van Trailer heads the 13.30 Newcastle to Kings Cross service. Also present are nos 56103, 37886 and 20903. Passenger numbers rose from 3.3m in 2002-3 to 4.4m in 2013-14. Westwood Bridge is in the background. (M.J.Stretton)

Other views of Peterborough can be seen in Middleton Press albums
Branch Lines around March, Branch Lines around Wisbech, Peterborough to Newark, Hitchin to Peterborough **and** *Peterborough to Kings Lynn.*

A DVD called *Peterborough to Lincoln* **is available from Middleton Press. It takes you on a silent cab ride in 2008, when much historic signalling was still in place.**

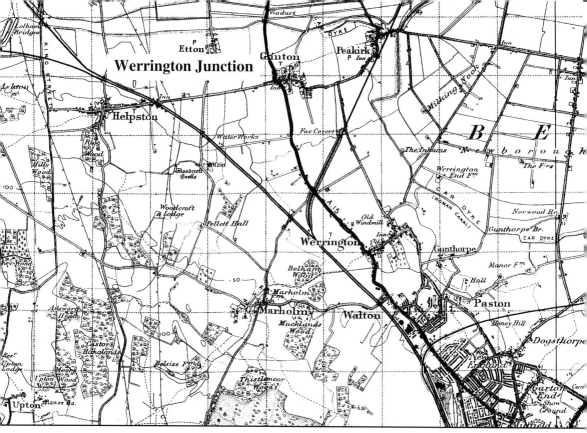

IV. The 1946 edition at 1ins to 1 mile has the New England Yard lower right and the main line to Doncaster running to the top left corner. The line to Sutton Bridge runs to the right border, having passed over the main line. The ex-MR line to Stamford curves to the left border and was independent of the main line at that time. Helpston station is marked and was open to passengers from 1846 to 1966. Its story appears in captions 33-34 in our *Peterborough to Newark* album. The first extra GNR line between New England and here was laid in 1866 and two more came in 1875, to add to the original double track.

13. Running north, about 10mm above the lower border of the map, in around 1900, is GNR 2-2-2 no. 873, with a mixture of GCR and GNR stock. The main line had water troughs north of the junction from about 1900 to 1960. (R.S.Carpenter)

Signal boxes	No. of levers	Opened	Closed
Crescent Junction	80	1874	1973
Peterborough North	30	1874	1972
Spital Junction	60	1873	1972
Eastfield	65	1893	-
Westwood	60	1873	1971
Werrington Junction	70	1891	1973

PEAKIRK

V. The 1901 edition is at 6ins to 1 mile. The station opened with the line as "Peakirk & Crowland". It became just Peakirk from 1857 to 1864 and again from 1871. The village housed 239 in 1901 and 238 in 1961. It is our last stop in the old Northants.

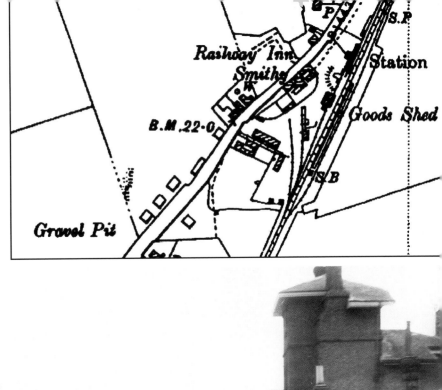

14. The platforms were staggered, so that passengers always crossed on the level. This undated southward view has a refuge siding on the left and the signal box in the distance. It was in use from 1922 until 27th May 1964.
(A.Harden coll.)

15. Closure to passengers took place on 11th September 1961 and to freight on 27th April 1964. This northward view is from 10th May 1958 and it includes a coal wagon. The building still stands, in use as a dwelling. Potatoes were the main items loaded, but wildfowl boxes were often put onto passenger trains.
(W.Taylor/
H.B.Priestley)

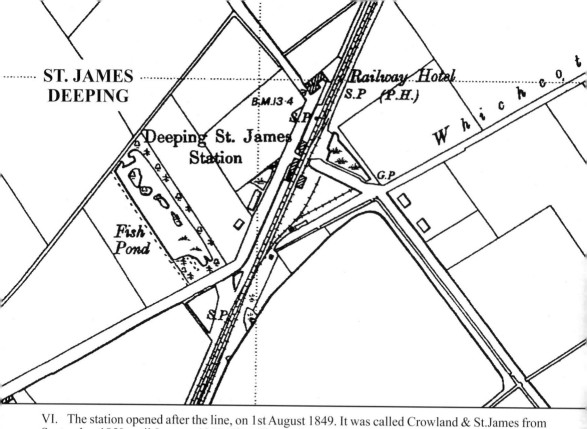

ST. JAMES DEEPING

Deeping St. James Station

Fish Pond

B.M.13·4

Railway Hotel
S.P (P.H.)

S.P.

G.P.

Whichcot

S.P.

VI.   The station opened after the line, on 1st August 1849. It was called Crowland & St.James from September 1850 until January 1851. The village of Deeping St.James is about one mile to the west and is one of a group called "The Deepings". The GNR had a brickworks nearby. The 1950 extract is at 12ins to 1 mile. Lower centre is a massive ballast pit.

16.   The railway reversed the words of the name, as shown on the signal box. A 1955 photograph emphasises the proximity of staff accommodation to two places of work. The box of 1876 had 32 levers and was in use until 3rd November 2014. The gates were worked by hand to the end of the life of the box. (Stations UK)

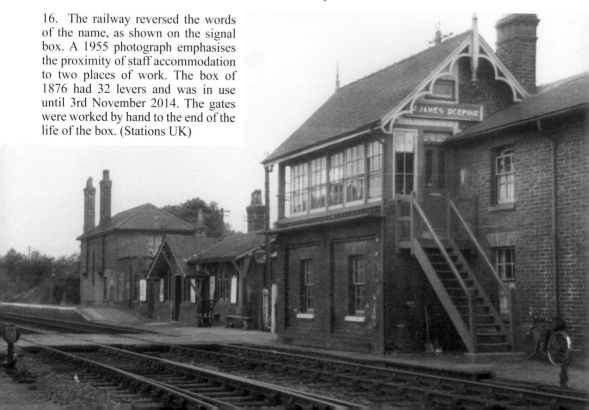

17. Here again, potatoes were the main items loaded. Goods traffic ceased here on 15th June 1964 and the goods shed was eventually demolished. The cottages were still occupied in the 21st century. (SLS coll.)

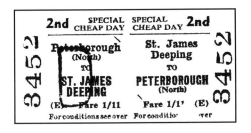

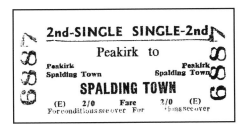

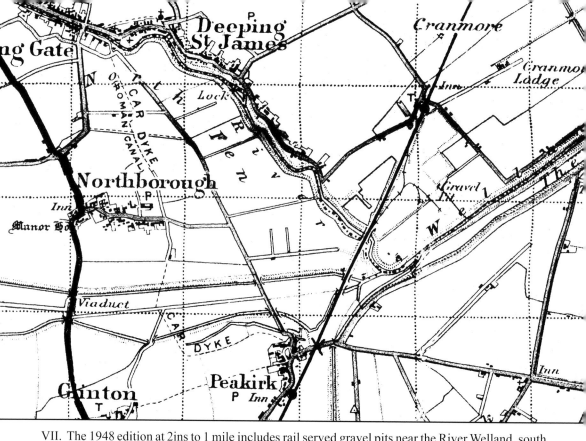

VII. The 1948 edition at 2ins to 1 mile includes rail served gravel pits near the River Welland, south of the station, which is top right. The gravel pits are now part of a nature reserve.

18. Passenger trains ceased to call after 11th September 1961, the year of this picture. The goods shed contained a 30cwt capacity crane, which was worked by hand. The open doors allowed wagons to be pushed up to the stops on the left. (Stations UK)

LITTLEWORTH

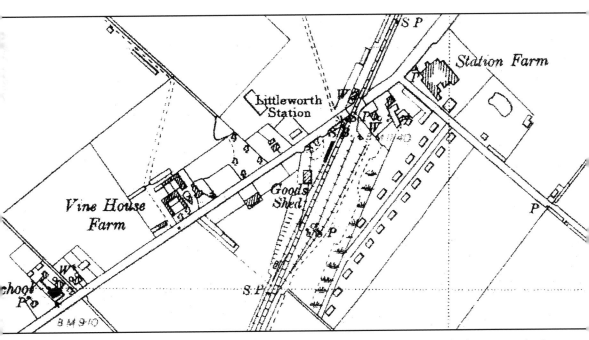

VIIIa.   This 1951 map is at 12ins to 1 mile. There had been an exchange siding in the area north of the level crossing, where potatoes were the main items loaded, from a narrow gauge line. It is just evident on the next map.

19.   A 1961 panorama has the level crossing in the distance and the station approach on the left. Passenger service ceased on 11th September of the same year. (Stations UK)

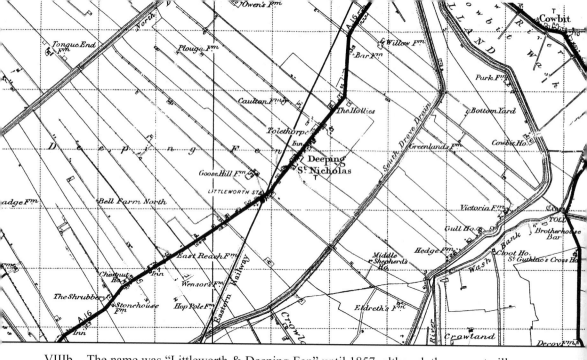

VIIIb.   The name was "Littleworth & Deeping Fen" until 1857, although the nearest village was Deeping St.Nicholas. It was on the main road, north of the station. The map is from 1946 and is at 1ins to 1 mile. With a lens one can find five tramways north of the A16 and two south of it. There had been eight and four. Only one ran to a private siding. It was that of W.Dennis & Sons, who laid 2ft gauge track in 1910, it reaching 11 miles by 1930. It closed in 1950.

20.   Coal wagons occupy the goods yard, which was in use until 15th June 1964. Potatoes were the largest outgoing crop and W.Dennis & Sons was the biggest producers locally. (Stations UK)

21. The 1875 box was photographed on 28th November 2013. It had a 30-lever frame and was in use until 3rd November 2014. The goods shed was also still standing at that time. Further north was the 12-lever Hawthorn Bank signal box from 1882 to 1966. This is near the lower border of the next map, by the bridge. (R.Geach)

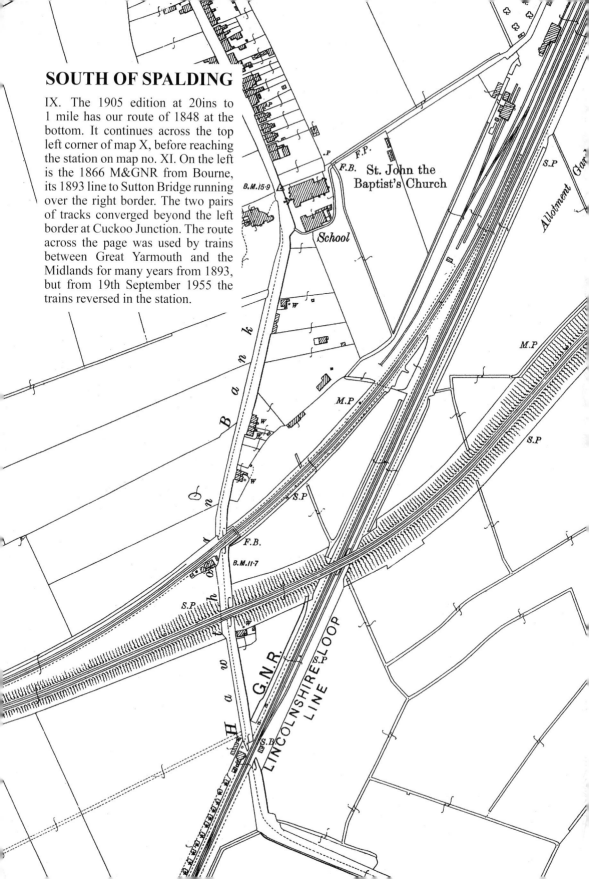

SOUTH OF SPALDING

IX. The 1905 edition at 20ins to 1 mile has our route of 1848 at the bottom. It continues across the top left corner of map X, before reaching the station on map no. XI. On the left is the 1866 M&GNR from Bourne, its 1893 line to Sutton Bridge running over the right border. The two pairs of tracks converged beyond the left border at Cuckoo Junction. The route across the page was used by trains between Great Yarmouth and the Midlands for many years from 1893, but from 19th September 1955 the trains reversed in the station.

St. John the Baptist's Church

F.P.

F.B.

B.M.15·9

P

S.P

Allotment Gar

School

W

M.P

M.P

S.P

S.P

B a n k

F.B.

B.M.11·7

S.P

S.P

O n

M.P

S.P

G.N.R.

LINCOLNSHIRE LOOP LINE

S.P

w a

H

S.B.

X. Rising from the lower border is the GNR/GER Joint line from March, which was in use from 1867 to 1982. The sharper curve from the M&GNR was open from 1858 to 1965. The route passes over the River Welland, which was navigable for a great distance and is lower right. Passenger service on the former M&GN route ceased on 28th February 1959, freight continuing until 1965.

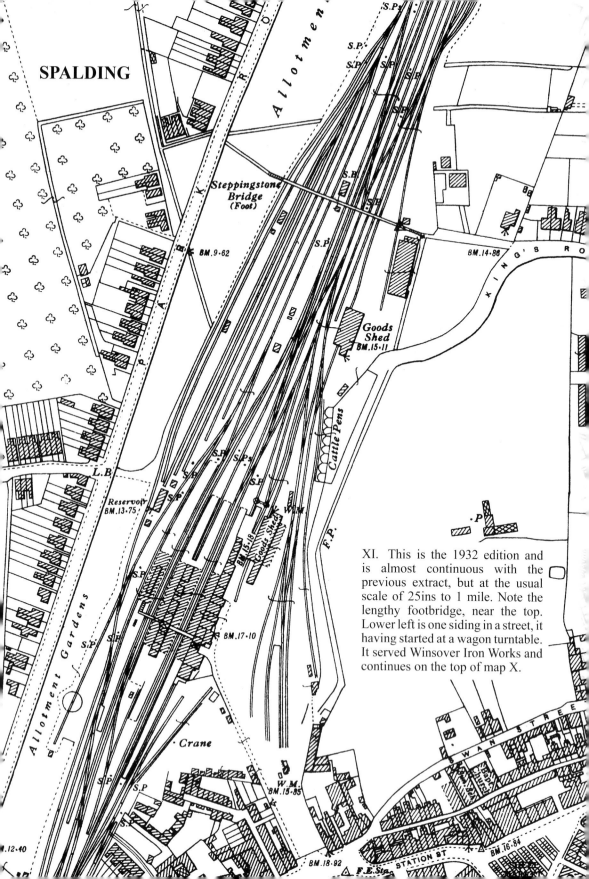

SPALDING

Steppingstone Bridge (Foot)

BM.9·62

Goods Shed
BM.15·11

Cattle Pens

S.P.

BM.14·86

KING'S RO

L.B.

Reservoir
BM.13·75

W.M.

Good Shed
BM.15·18

·P

F.P.

BM.17·10

Allotment Gardens

Crane

W.M.
BM.15·85

·S.P.

S.P.

XI. This is the 1932 edition and is almost continuous with the previous extract, but at the usual scale of 25ins to 1 mile. Note the lengthy footbridge, near the top. Lower left is one siding in a street, it having started at a wagon turntable. It served Winsover Iron Works and continues on the top of map X.

SWAN STREE

STATION ST

BM.16·84

.12·40

BM.18·92

F.E.Sta.

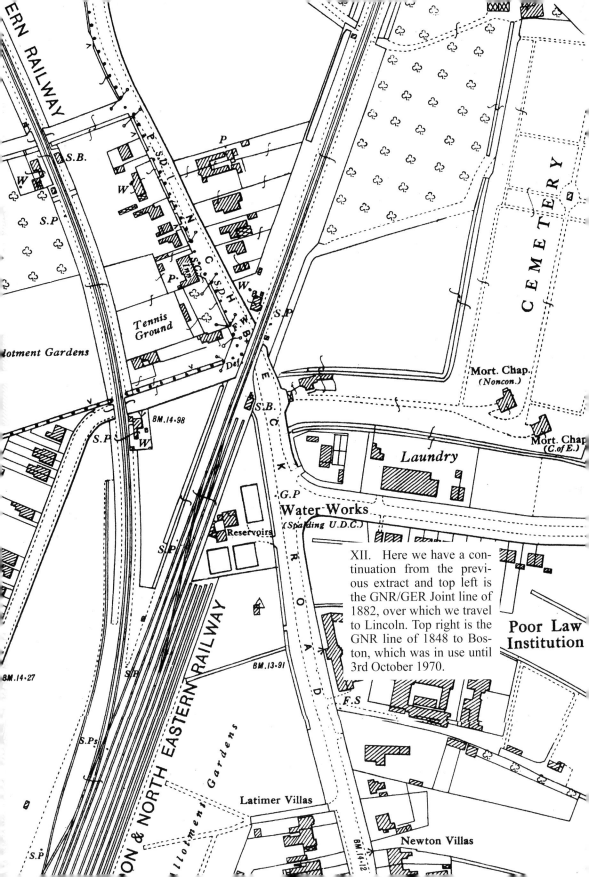

ERN RAILWAY

S.B.

W

S.P

Allotment Gardens

P

W

P.

Tennis Ground

FW

Def.

BM.14·98

W

S.P

BM.14·27

S.P

S.Ps

LONDON & NORTH EASTERN RAILWAY

Allotment Gardens

Reservoirs

S.P

S.P

BM.13·91

GREAT NORTHERN JOINT COMMITTEE

S.B.

S.P

W

P

S.P

S.B.

G.P

Water Works
(Spalding U.D.C.)

CEMETERY

Mort. Chap.
(Noncon.)

Mort. Chap.
(C.of E.)

Laundry

XII.   Here we have a continuation from the previous extract and top left is the GNR/GER Joint line of 1882, over which we travel to Lincoln. Top right is the GNR line of 1848 to Boston, which was in use until 3rd October 1970.

Poor Law
Institution

F.S

BM.14·12

Latimer Villas

Newton Villas

22.   Ready to depart south is M&GNR 4-4-0 no. 7. The card's post mark was 1913. The station was considered to be on a main line until the Grimsby traffic ceased on 3rd October 1970. However, the Harwich boat trains continued to pass through until 7th May 1973. (P.Laming coll.)

23.   The small engine shed was photographed on 27th May 1937. It opened on 1st August 1866, having been built by the MR. It was also used by the GNR from 1868 and owned jointly by them from around 1895. It became a sub-shed of New England (35A) in 1949 and Boston (40F) in 1958. Closure came on 7th March 1960. The shed is near the top of map IX. (H.C.Casserley)

24.   It is 16th April 1947 and class K3 2-6-0 no. 1849 runs into the station from the north. The long Steppingstone Bridge is in the background and close to us is the barrow crossing. The perforated concrete signal post was a M&GN patent, which was sold to its parent company. (H.C.Casserley)

25.   The east bound M&GN train from Leicester has arrived and the replacement engine is now ready to depart. It is class 4MT 2-6-0 no. 43161. The incoming engine has run round and waits on the left to go to its depot. (W.A.Camwell/SLS)

26.   A southward view in 1956-57 has another class 4MT, no. 43086, on M&GN duties. This old term lingered on in staff parlance until the route closed. No. 1 Box is on the right. Its 80-lever frame was in use from 1920 until 22nd July 1984, when resignalling took place. The same details apply to No. 2, which was at the north end of the station. On the latter date, No. 1 was fitted with a panel and No. 2 box closed. Resignalling took place again on 3rd November 2014 and the line was controlled from Lincoln. There were six boxes from 1882 to 1920. (Milepost 92½)

27.   The suffix TOWN was used from 1948 to 1968. Class J6 0-6-0 no. 64192 stands at Platform 2 with a southbound freight in the mid-1950s. No. 1 is the bay platform on the right. (Milepost 92½)

28.   Sugar beet traffic was heavy for many decades, but it ceased in 1980, when the factory on the Boston line closed. Vans stand in Platform 1 as a reminder of the immense flower traffic that was loaded there every Summer evening, in the past. (Milepost 92½)

29.   A northward panorama from 3rd May 1969 includes one of the goods sheds. The yard had closed on 4th July 1966, having become a coal depot only on 2nd August 1965. There had been a locomotive turntable at the south end of the left yard until the end of steam. The bay platform in the centre had been numbered 4. (Milepost 92½)

30.   Southbound on 8th October 1976 is no. 40067 with a mixed freight. A few point rods remain on the ballast after much rationalisation. This is the view from the footbridge at Winsover Road, shown at the top of map X. (T.Heavyside)

31.   Seen on the same day from Steppingstone Bridge is a DMU working the 14.13 Cambridge to Doncaster service. Four platforms were still in use. (T.Heavyside)

32. The flags are out for the popular Spalding Flower Parade on 9th May 1981. No. 37090 (right) was working a special from Shoeburyness. The other trains that day were from: Lichfield (47474), Hull/Cleethorpes (DMU), Keighley (40034), London Kings Cross (47520), Crewe (47462), Norwich (47535), Kemble (47142), Shrewsbury (46002), Oxford (47119), Bristol (47061), Newcastle (47094), Weston Super Mare (47041), Cardiff (47579), Swansea (47137), Poole (47562), Morpeth (46036), Settle (40078), Tonbridge (47569), Yeovil (47049) and Manchester Piccadilly (47471). There was also a Yarmouth-Newcastle train each way, plus the local trains. (R.Geach)

33. We move to 16th October 2010 and witness an East Coast Main Line diversion, hauled by no. 43313. The Festival trains ceased in the late 1980s and the seven berthing sidings were taken out of use. (J.Whitehouse)

34. No. 156415 is working a Lincoln to Peterborough service on 3rd November 2012. Platform 1 (right) could take nine coaches, while No. 2 was fit for seven. (P.Jones)

For other views see *Branch Lines around Spalding* **and** *Spalding to Grimsby* **albums from Middleton Press.**

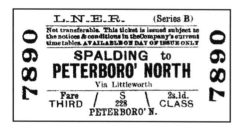

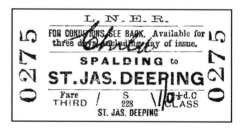

NORTH OF SPALDING

35. Our route to Lincoln curves to the left, while the former Boston line continues straight into the distance. This DMU is working from Doncaster to Cambridge on 8th October 1976. The sidings on the right were retained into the 21st century. (T.Heavyside)

36. Mill Green Crossing was ½ mile north of the station and it retained its 1882 21-lever box until 11th August 2014, when it was closed. Barriers had arrived. The gates had been worked by a wheel. (R.Geach)

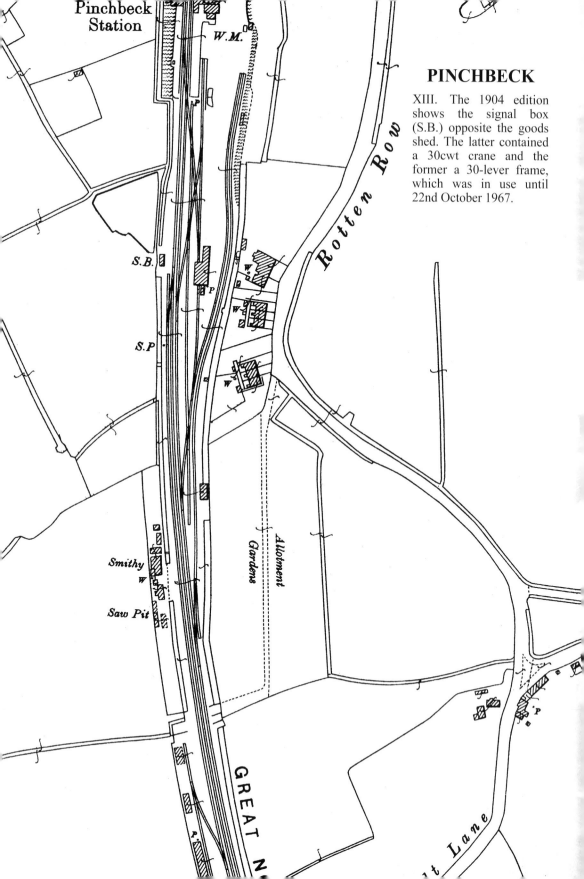

Pinchbeck
Station

W.M.

PINCHBECK

XIII. The 1904 edition
shows the signal box
(S.B.) opposite the goods
shed. The latter contained
a 30cwt crane and the
former a 30-lever frame,
which was in use until
22nd October 1967.

Rotten Row

S.B.

S.P.

Allotment

Gardens

Smithy

W

Saw Pit

GREAT N

t Lane

37. An early postcard producer invited a porter to give the impression that a sack truck would be used to unload a goods train. The village was nearby and it housed 2830 folk in 1901 and 3826 in 1961. (LOSA)

38. A later postcard included more of the staff, plus another goods train, plus the up inner home signal. The architectural details were to a high standard on this 1882 route. (LOSA)

39. A 1959 view reveals loss of canopies and a general air of decay. Closure took place on 11th September 1961. Freight service was withdrawn on 7th December 1964. (Stations UK)

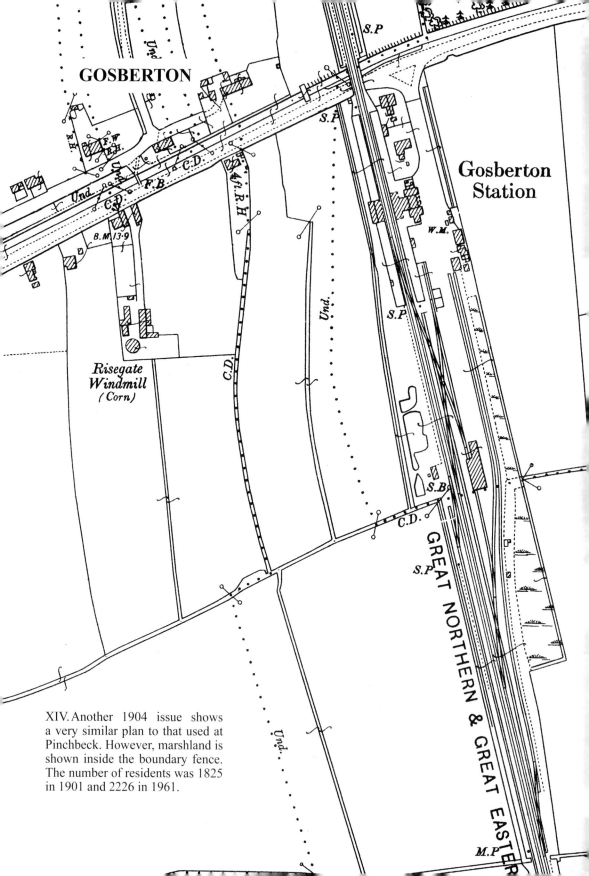

GOSBERTON

Und.

S.P

S.P

**Gosberton
Station**

R.H.

F.W
E.H.

C.D.

F.B

4½.R.H.

W.M.

C.D.

B.M.13·9

Und.

S.P.

*Risegate
Windmill
(Corn)*

C.D.

Und.

S.B.

C.D.

S.P

GREAT NORTHERN & GREAT EASTER

Und.

XIV. Another 1904 issue shows
a very similar plan to that used at
Pinchbeck. However, marshland is
shown inside the boundary fence.
The number of residents was 1825
in 1901 and 2226 in 1961.

M.P

40. An early postcard shows that canopy repairs had already been required. Track repairs by hand were always ongoing. (LOSA)

41. A 1960 pair of pictures reveal loss of weather protection and wild plant growth beginning. Staff accommodation is included in both. Both closure dates are as for Pinchbeck. (Stations UK)

42. The 1882 signal box is evident here. Its 30-lever frame was worked until 19th March 2012, when a Portakabin was provided. It contained a panel which was used until 11th August 2014, when the new Lincoln Signalling Control Centre took over the route. (Stations UK)

DONINGTON ROAD

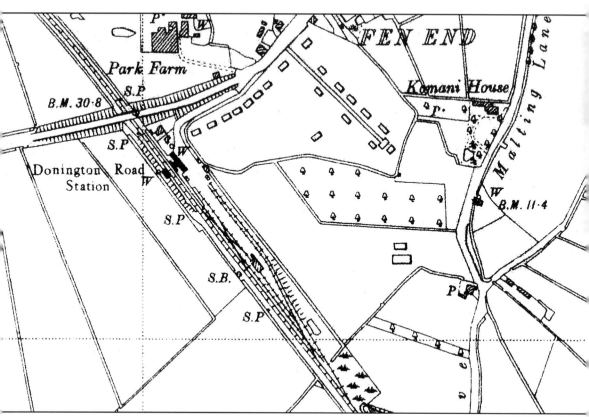

XV. The station was at the west end of the village only ½ mile from its centre. It housed 1486 in 1901 and 1948 in 1961. The 1950 edition is at 12ins to 1 mile.

43.   Almost all the railway property of 1882 is included in this panorama. It emphasises the road debris problem of the horse transport era. However, the droppings were of value in the gardens and were often collected, by the lower orders, mainly. (LOSA)

44. The architecture has become familiar and so have the closure dates - passengers 11th September 1961 and freight 7th December 1964. There had been a siding 1½ miles to the south, at Quadring. Its 21-lever signal box was usable from 1900 to 5th October 1966. (P.Laming coll.)

45. The property survey is completed in this 1960 view, even the signal box can be glimpsed between the ladder rungs. It had 30 levers and lasted in use until 2nd October 1977. The location gained fame in 2008 when Hull Trains proposed that it should become Donington Parkway, for trains on its planned Grimsby-Lincoln-London service. (Stations UK)

HELPRINGHAM

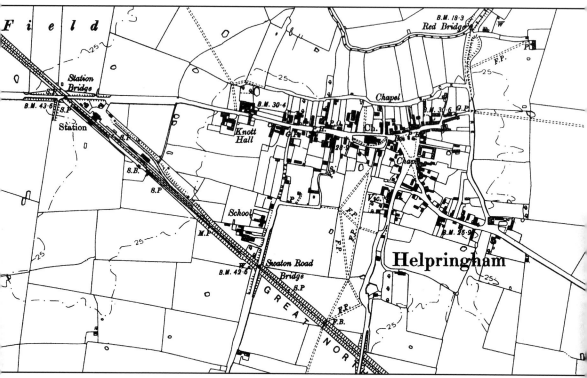

XVI.   The 1906 survey is at 6ins to 1 mile. The village housed 767 folk in 1901 and 671 in 1961.

46. The 1882 structures can be enjoyed again, as a freight train approaches. That service was discontinued here on 7th December 1964. Closure to passengers came early, on 4th July 1955. (LOSA)

47.   Seen in 1960 are most of the buildings, although the box is in line with the signal post. It had 30 levers and closed on 4th October 1982. About two miles to the south was Blotoft Box, which had 16 levers, in use until closure on 11th August 2014. (Stations UK)

SLEAFORD   Holdingham

Anna House

St. Mary's Chapel (Site of)

Poplar Farm

Jolly Scotchman (P.H.)

Lincoln 16
Sleaford 1 } M.P.

INGHAM

Northfield Farm

XVII.   The 1906 edition is
scaled at 6ins to 1 mile and
has the direct curve north on
the right page. It was in use
from 1882 until 1985 and
again from 2013. The east-
west route is annotated and is
still in use. The left of the two
lines at the lower border was
to Bourne for passengers,
until 22nd September 1930,
and ran to Billingborough for
freight, until 1956.

Claremont Place

N E W

Galley Hill Bridge

Galley Hill Plantation

GREAT NORTHERN & GREAT EASTERN JOINT RAILWAY

Galley Hill

Catchwater Drain

Drove Lane

Drove Lane Bridge

Galley Hill Farm   *The Wilderness*

Carre's Gr[...] School
(Carre's [...])

S L E A F O R D   U. D.

Bouncing Hill

Sleaford Drain

Sleaford Fen

Sock Drain

Manor House

Guildhall Springs

Fen Drove

Watercress Beds

Cobbler's Hole (Spring)

Clay Hill

Sleaford Water Works

Nine Foot River

G.N.R.

Castle (Site of)
Moat
Castle Field

SLEAFORD

Alexandra St.

GRANTHAM, SLEAFORD & BOSTON

Sleaford West Junction

Hospital (Infectious Diseases)

Station

School

Reservoir (Sleaford Water Works)

NEW QUARRINGTON

Crick Grou[...]

Quarrington   Hill

Bullock Pasture

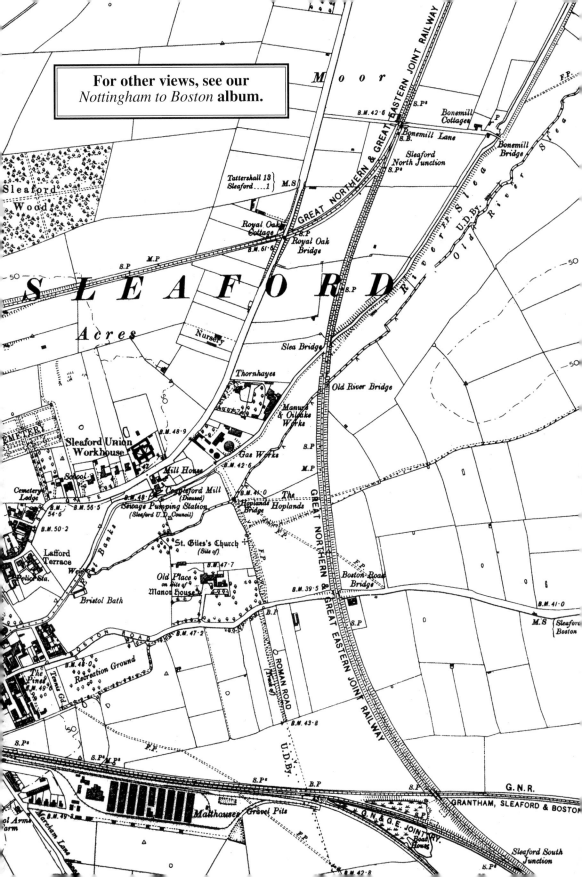

For other views, see our
Nottingham to Boston **album.**

M o o r

GREAT NORTHERN & GREAT EASTERN JOINT RAILWAY

B.M. 42.6

S.P.

Bonemill
Cottages

Bonemill Lane

Bonemill
Bridge

Sleaford
North Junction

S.P.

Tattershall 13
Sleaford 1   M.S

River F.P. Slea

U.D.By.

Old River Slea

Royal Oak
Cottage

S.P.

Royal Oak
Bridge

GREAT NORTHERN &

B.M. 61.0

50

S.P.   M.P

S.P.

50

S L E A F O R D

A c r e s

Nursery

Slea Bridge

Thornhayes

Old River Bridge

Manure
& Oilcake
Works

S.P.

M.P

B.M. 48.9

CEMETERY

Sleaford Union
Workhouse

School

Cemetery
Lodge

B.M.
54.6   B.M. 56.5

B.M. 50.2

Mill House

Castleford Mill
(Disused)

B.M. 48.

Sewage Pumping Station
(Sleaford U.D. Council)

Gas Works

B.M. 42.6

B.M. 41.0

Hoplands
Bridge

The
Hoplands

GREAT NORTHERN &

Lafford
Terrace

Police Sta.

West Banks

Bristol Bath

St. Giles's Church
(Site of)

B.M. 47.7

Old Place
on Site of
Manor House

Boston Road
Bridge

B.M. 39.5

S.P.

B.M. 41.0

M.S   Sleaford
Boston

BOSTON ROAD

B.M. 47.2

The
Pines

B.M. 49.6

Tennis Gd.

Recreation Ground

ROMAN ROAD
(Course of)

B.P.

GREAT EASTERN JOINT RAILWAY

B.M. 43.8

U.D.By.

S.P.

F.P.

S.P.   M.P.

B.P.

G.N.R.

Malthouse   Gravel Pits

GRANTHAM, SLEAFORD & BOSTON

l Arms
arm

Mareham Lane Bridge

G.N. & G.E. JOINT RLY.

Boat
House

Sleaford South
Junction

B.M. 42.8

S.P.

48.   A train is departing for Boston and is passing East box. At least ten eyes are watching on the left, including the horse's. Above are GNR somersault signals. (LOSA)

49.   A view in the other direction includes the same signals, but their bracket had been upgraded. The speed limit has been emphasised by a dark-leaved bush. The 4-4-0 is the LNER class D3 no. 4311 and is running in from Boston. (SLS coll.)

50. We are still close to East Box (left) and find two horse boxes nearby. There is a second water column and tank at the far end of Platform 2. No. 3 is on the left in this 1948 view. (Stations UK)

51. We gain a good view of the goods shed office in about 1956, but not any train details. The locomotive is class B2 4-6-0 no. 61635 *Milton* and it is probably bound for Great Yarmouth, judging by the number of coaches. (C.L.Caddy coll.)

52. A 1960 panorama includes East box; its gates are across the tracks. The location was the last place to retain a signal box on all four points of the compass. Our journey was close to all four until 2014, when the number diminished. (Stations UK)

53. Running in from the east on 8th October 1976 is no. 31102, with a pick-up freight from Boston. The signals allowed access to both "Main" and "Back" platforms. (T.Heavyside)

54. A short while later, the same engine was recorded shunting the south yard. Included is West Box and its massive rodding tunnel. The south yard was called "West Yard", because it was entered from West Box. The goods shed is in the background and the window cleaner's platform is top right. (T.Heavyside)

55. No. 31298 is seen with a Leeds to Yarmouth train in August 1983. The roof and glazing on the footbridge were removed later. The ventilators on the right were above the facilities for gentlemen. Most trains used Platform 1 after the 2014 resignalling. (J.Whitehouse)

56. No. 156413 is working from Nottingham to Skegness on 10th February 2012. East Box had its 50-lever frame replaced by a panel in 2011, hence the colour light signals. There were over 0.3m passengers using the station annually in the period 2004-15. (P.Jones)

57. Later the next day, we find West Box in the distance; its 57-lever frame had the number reduced to 46 in 1965. South Box is not illustrated. The 1882 building had its 16 levers in use until 30th December 1957. A new flat-roofed one then opened. It had 25 levers and was in use until 14th April 2014, when Lincoln took over. (P.Jones)

XVIIIa. The branch to the Royal Air Force station is shown top left on this 1947 survey at 6ins to 1 mile. It did not appear on earlier editions for security reasons. The camp opened in 1914 and was initially used by the Royal Flying Corps and the Royal Naval Air Service; the latter operated airships here. The line opened in 1916. The RAF was formed in 1918, when the connection at Sleaford was made. The line ceased to be used in August 1956.

XVIIIb. This map is the 1954 edition at 1ins to 1 mile, which takes the branch to the camp boundary. It also includes the Sleaford Avoiding Line to the right of the town.

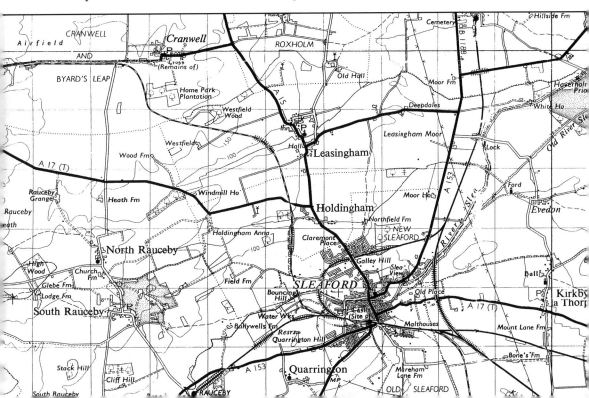

58.   This is the terminus in about 1918. There were usually eight passenger trains each weekday, with four on Sundays. There was a platform at Slea Bridge, for use when short workings were necessary. The bridge is near the words Sleaford Fen on the map. There were no regular passenger trains after 1927, when buses took over the traffic. (RAF College Cranwell coll.)

XIX The line was just over five miles long and this is its terminus at its optimum. The engine shed is top left. The line continued further north to the airship hangar, until about 1923. (RAF College Cranwell coll.)

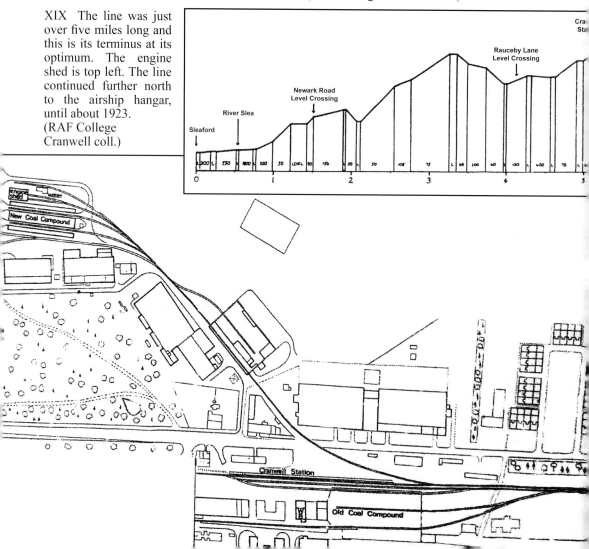

59. A photograph from 1919 reveals that ex-GNR four-wheeled coaches were often used for the short journey. There were also a few six-wheelers. Also seen is 0-6-0ST no. 7 *Bletcher*, which was built by Manning Wardle as no. 318 in 1870. It was on the line in 1919-34 and had earlier worked for the contractor who built the branch. Eight-coach trains were common in the early years. (RAF College Cranwell coll.)

60. This is the East Camp crossing on 19th July 1949 and only the Austin 7 suffered injury, despite being lightly constructed. The front wheels had only three studs and were prone to come loose. (Your author, Vic Mitchell, was overtaken by one such wheel at red traffic lights in 1951.) Many locomotives had short stays on the branch and some were hired from the LNER or BR. (RAF College Cranwell coll.)

61. A Coronation special from Kensington Olympia ran in June 1953 and was hauled from Sleaford by class J6 0-6-0 no. 64196. For many years after World War II, there was just one return goods train, Mondays to Fridays only. There were three exchange sidings at the start of the branch.
(RAF College Cranwell coll.)

62.   We are looking south on 8th October 1979 as the 10.56 Cambridge to Doncaster leaves the curve. Behind it is the straight track of the Sleaford Avoiding Line, which was out of use from 1985 to 2013. (T.Heavyside)

63.   On the same curve on 7th December 2013 is class 7P 4-6-2 no. 70013 *Oliver Cromwell*, with "The Gresley Society Golden Jubilee" on its headboard. In the foreground is equipment for the new signalling, which would result in closure of the 18-lever box on 14th April 2014. The gates were worked manually, until barriers arrived. One old post is evident. The curve was single by that time. (J.Whitehouse)

RUSKINGTON

Later Works
Ruskington U.D.C.)

Manor House

All Saints' Church

Rectory

The Elms

Ruskington

Alliance Cottages

Chapel

M.P

F.B.

S.P

S.P

Sta.

S.P

Goods S.

S.P.

RUSKINGTON CEMETERY

XX. The population in 1901 was 1196, rising to 2462 by 1961. The 1949 edition is scaled at 12ins to 1 mile and shows a stream along the centre of the High Street.

64. An early postcard reveals that the up side had a heated waiting room and a cast iron urinal for gentlemen, on the right. (LOSA)

65.   This record includes the track gang as well as the staff, the latter being in uniform with polished buttons. The incomplete valance painting is difficult to explain. (LOSA)

66.   The 12.54pm (SO) Doncaster to March pauses for parcels and photographers, according to one of the latter. Class V2 2-6-2 no. 60870 is simmering nicely, on 18th February 1961. Passenger service ceased here on 11th September 1961, but only for 14 years. (J.Langford)

67. A panoramic view from the road bridge in 1961 confirms that there was no footbridge. In the distance is the goods yard, which closed on 7th December 1964; it contained a 10-ton crane. The signal box had 30 levers and continued in use until 23rd May 1982. The goods shed stood even longer. (Stations UK)

68. An entirely new station was available from 5th May 1975 and is seen in March 2010. Both platforms were designed to take three cars, but were devoid of a linking footbridge until 2014. There were two shelters and a free car park. Passenger numbers varied greatly between 109,000 in 2006 and 85,000 in 2012. (R.Geach)

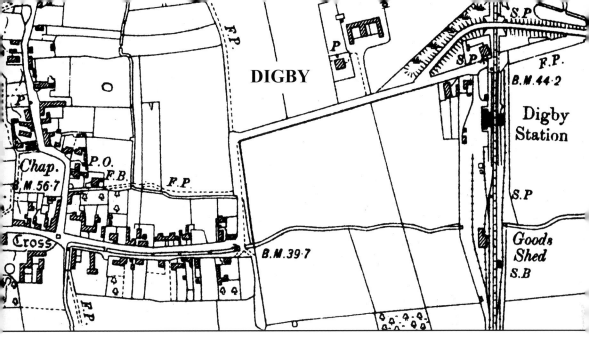

DIGBY

Chap.
B.M.56·7

P.O.
F.B.

F.P.

Cross

F.P.

B.M.39·7

F.P.

B.M.44·2

Digby
Station

S.P

Good's
Shed
S.B

XXI. The 1906 edition is at 12ins to 1 mile and it includes the village centre. Its residents numbered 351 in 1901 and 426 in 1961. There were two private sidings nearby listed in 1938; south of the station was one for the Dorrington Hide and Skin Company.

69. A 1955 view features an up freight train approaching the staff crossing, which was unusual in having a white outline to its step. This was probably added during the black-out days of World War II. (Stations UK)

70. Seen in 1961 is the 34-lever signal box, which lasted until 14th November 1971. The goods yard, opposite, closed on 15th June 1964. Passenger service had ceased on 11th September 1961. Further south had been Bloxholme siding, another private one. (Stations UK)

SCOPWICK & TIMBERLAND

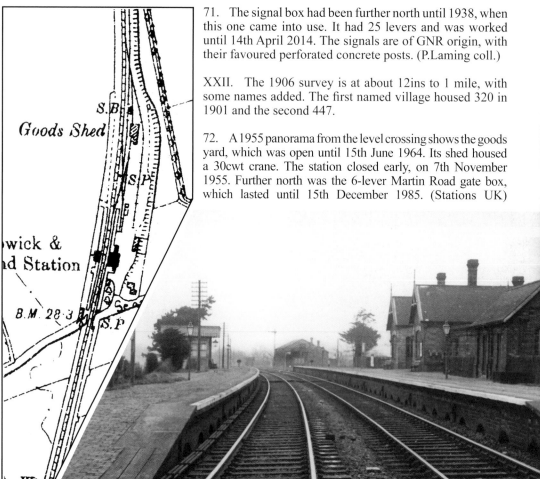

71.   The signal box had been further north until 1938, when this one came into use. It had 25 levers and was worked until 14th April 2014. The signals are of GNR origin, with their favoured perforated concrete posts. (P.Laming coll.)

XXII.   The 1906 survey is at about 12ins to 1 mile, with some names added. The first named village housed 320 in 1901 and the second 447.

72.   A 1955 panorama from the level crossing shows the goods yard, which was open until 15th June 1964. Its shed housed a 30cwt crane. The station closed early, on 7th November 1955. Further north was the 6-lever Martin Road gate box, which lasted until 15th December 1985. (Stations UK)

The Grange

Allotments

BLANKNEY & METHERINGHAM

Metheringham

Goods Shed

Sewage Works
(Branston R.D.C.)

Blankney & Metheringham
Station

Filter Beds

Filter Bed

Tank

Farm

Umber Yard

Hall Garth

Moat

Sluice

S.P.

XXIII. The 1907 issue is at about 25ins to 1 mile. Blankney and its large park is around one mile to the south. Both tree-lined drives to it begin at the lower border. Its importance thus gave the name priority.

73. Full architectural detail was provided and the extension behind the name board gave extensive facilities for gentlemen. The first signal box is at the far end of the opposite platform. Metheringham was home to 1517 folk in 1901 and 1679 in 1961. (LOSA)

74. A 1961 view includes the 1928 box, which was built adjacent to the level crossing. The canopies had vanished, but the goods shed can still be seen. The station closed on 11th September 1961 and the goods yard followed on 15th June 1964. (Stations UK)

METHERINGHAM

75. The station was reopened on 6th October 1975, using the most helpful name. The use of timber minimised the weight on the soft Fenland ground. The 1976 timetable showed seven down trains calling and eight up, weekdays only. (D.A.Thompson)

76. The 1928 30-lever box was photographed on 2nd November 2012, still retaining its original name of Blankney. The signalman still moved the gates by wheel. The box closed on 14th April 2014. (P.Jones)

77. No. 153374 waits to depart on the same day, while working from Peterborough to Lincoln. Near the fences are yellow boxes containing grit for use on icy days. (P.Jones)

78. A view towards Lincoln on 22nd April 2015 records this signal free scene, with a rusty crossover and siding in the distance. There was another disused siding behind the camera, on the down side. (Janet Smith)

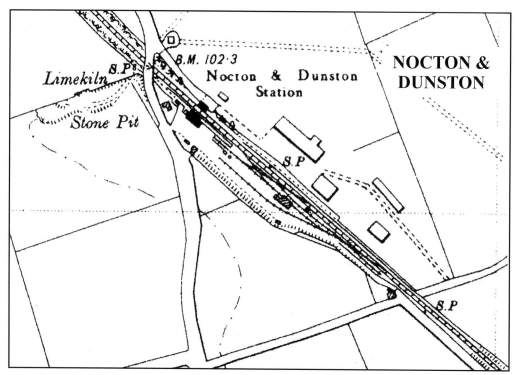

XXIV. The 1949 survey is reproduced at 12ins to 1 mile. The population of Nocton was 482 in 1901 and Dunston was 572. The four buildings on the right had earlier been involved with the potato traffic. The biggest one is seen in picture 82.

79. The original architectural details can be enjoyed, but the canopies were not long-lived. They are not in the next picture. Passenger service ceased early, closure coming on 2nd May 1955. (LOSA)

80.   A southward panorama from about 1939 shows points on the left, which served the loop seen in picture 82. It was a private siding, with gates at each end. (Stations UK)

81.   This 1961 record presents a sad scene, but the goods yard remained in use until 15th June 1964. Its goods shed contained a 30cwt crane. The 27-lever signal box functioned until 9th May 1965. (Stations UK)

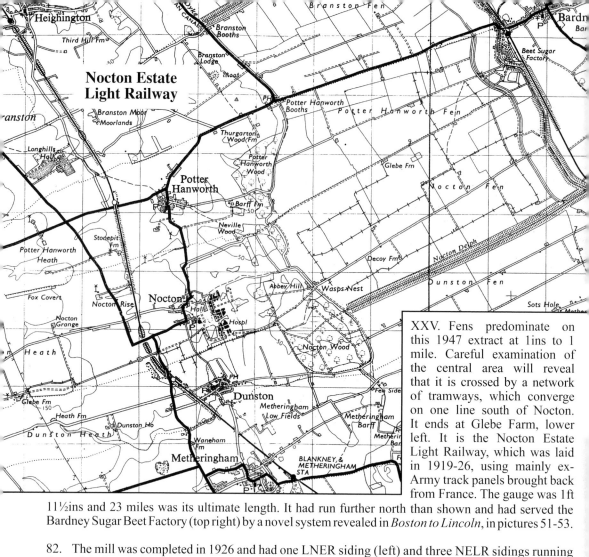

Nocton Estate Light Railway

XXV. Fens predominate on this 1947 extract at 1ins to 1 mile. Careful examination of the central area will reveal that it is crossed by a network of tramways, which converge on one line south of Nocton. It ends at Glebe Farm, lower left. It is the Nocton Estate Light Railway, which was laid in 1919-26, using mainly ex-Army track panels brought back from France. The gauge was 1ft 11½ins and 23 miles was its ultimate length. It had run further north than shown and had served the Bardney Sugar Beet Factory (top right) by a novel system revealed in *Boston to Lincoln*, in pictures 51-53.

82. The mill was completed in 1926 and had one LNER siding (left) and three NELR sidings running through it. Seen in 1956 is one of its six Simplex locomotives, built by Motor Rail. This is their no. 1935, which was built in 1920 and converted from petrol to diesel in 1934. The bogie wagons are part of a fleet of 53 bought from the Army. Also purchased were 32 four-wheelers and 12 ambulance vans. Later, four tank wagons were bought for drinking water distribution and seven side tippers for ballast. (A.Neale coll.)

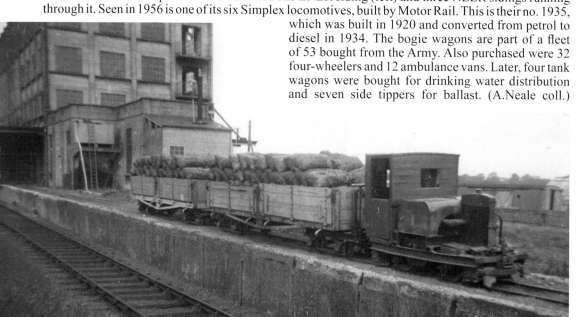

83. Fowler 0-6-0T no. 16991 was photographed outside its maker's works on 4th October 1926. It was the only steam locomotive on the line and proved too heavy for the portable track. It was sold for use in Durham in about 1931. Many of the potatoes went to Lincoln by road to become Smiths Crisps. (A.Neale coll.)

84. No. 6 was Motor Rail no. 3652 of 1924 and is seen on 25th July 1951 at the exchange sidings. This also had an engine change to diesel. Two ambulance vans are in the background, plus one Hudson bogie wagon. Your scribe, Vic Mitchell, helped load two of these onto a lorry in 1959, while a director of the Festiniog Railway Society and a National Service Officer. The RAF records showed "crane driver's training exercise", but he seemed skilled.
(B.Roberts/A.Neale)

85. No. 5 was Motor Rail no. 3995 of 1934 and it is seen on 15th May 1955, hauling a coach built on the estate. The faint headboard was intended to reveal the presence of the Narrow Gauge Railway Society. The points are at Wasps Nest (see map) and the siding leads to the ballast quarry. The coaches were often used for shooting parties around the estate. (K.E.Hartley/A.Neale)

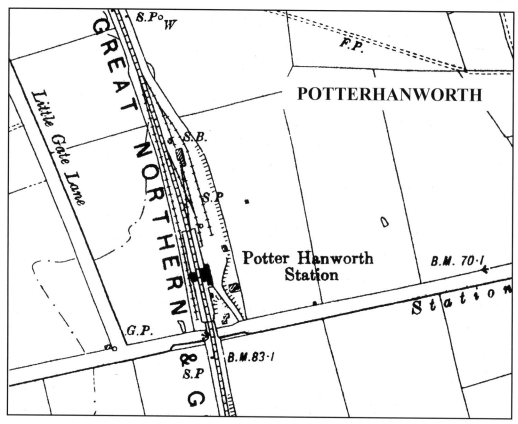

XXVI. The 1901 map at 12ins to 1 mile shows the name as two words, but in most railway use it was one. The village was ½ mile to the east and housed only 480 in 1901.

86. We have two northward views for comparison. This card includes the goods yard, which was in use until 15th June 1964. Passenger service ended here on 2nd May 1955. (LOSA)

87. This scene is from about 1930, but we have no details about the train. Above the rear of it is the top of the signal box, which had 32 levers and was in use until 24th March 1996. (Stations UK)

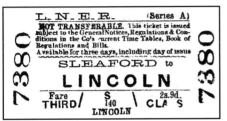

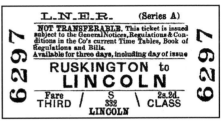

BRANSTON & HEIGHINGTON

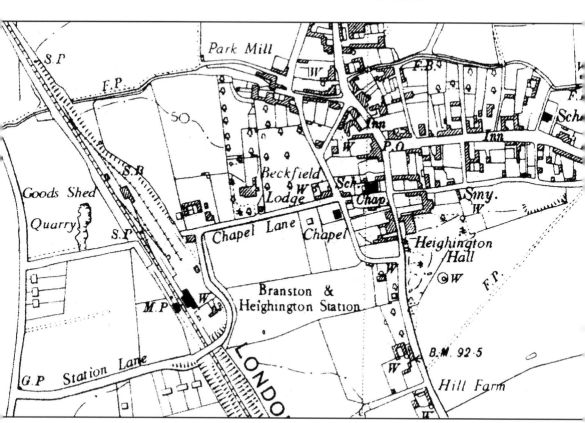

XXVII. The 1949 survey at 12ins to 1 mile shows the close proximity of the station to Heighington. Branston was over a mile to the south. In 1901, the former housed 655 and the latter 1216.

88. An early view features the usual generous weather protection. For the first two years of the life of the station, its names were in the reverse order. Passenger service continued until 3rd November 1958. (P.Laming coll.)

89.   Another northward panorama and this is from about 1930. In the distance is the small signal box, which had 24 levers and closed on 15th February 1976. The nearby goods yard lasted until 7th December 1964. Half a mile north of the station is the 60yd long Cross Roads Tunnel. The roads are above. (Stations UK)

EAST OF LINCOLN

XXVIII. The 1898 survey at 1ins to 1 mile is helpful to identify the radiating routes. Top right is the line to Market Rasen. Below it is the Boston line, drawn within the banks of the River Witham. A short link of single track to the Peterborough route is shown. This was later doubled. Curving south is the Navenby route and lower left is the one to Nottingham. Top left are lines to Chesterfield and Gainsborough. The freight bypass route is shown with a hatched light line.

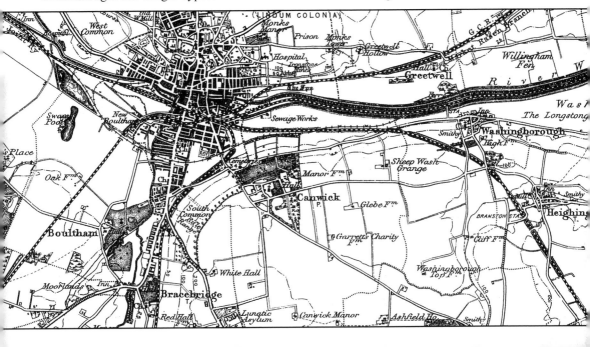

XXIX. Seen at 6ins to 1 mile in 1930, the river runs across the scene, south of the historic city centre, which is on high ground. Lower left is the ex-MR station, which closed to passengers in 1985, its freight yard lasting to 1965. Further north are the ex-GNR premises, which are described herein. Its engine shed was rescued from demolition in 2000.

➔ 90. This crossing is clear on the second map, the ex-GCR rails being across the picture, which is from 7th October 1976. No. 31263 is running in from Sleaford, with empty stock. On the right is Pelham Street signal box of 1874; it had 100 levers. In the distance is Sincil Bank box of 1882; it had 42. (T.Heavyside)

91.   Seen on the same day is the 17.16 Boston to Lincoln (left) and the 17.12 Doncaster to Sleaford (right). The left box closed on 29th January 1984 and the other lasted until 11th July 2008, when Lincoln Signalling Centre came into use. It is east hereof. (T.Heavyside)

92.   Single car no. 153308 passes Pelham Street Junction box on the approach to Lincoln with a train from Peterborough via Sleaford on 1st April 2008. The train is passing the spot where the Cleethorpes-Newark line once crossed the route from Sleaford on the level. The sidings in the background remained in use as a loading point for scrap metal bound for Cardiff. Workers are busy with new wiring. (P.D.Shannon)

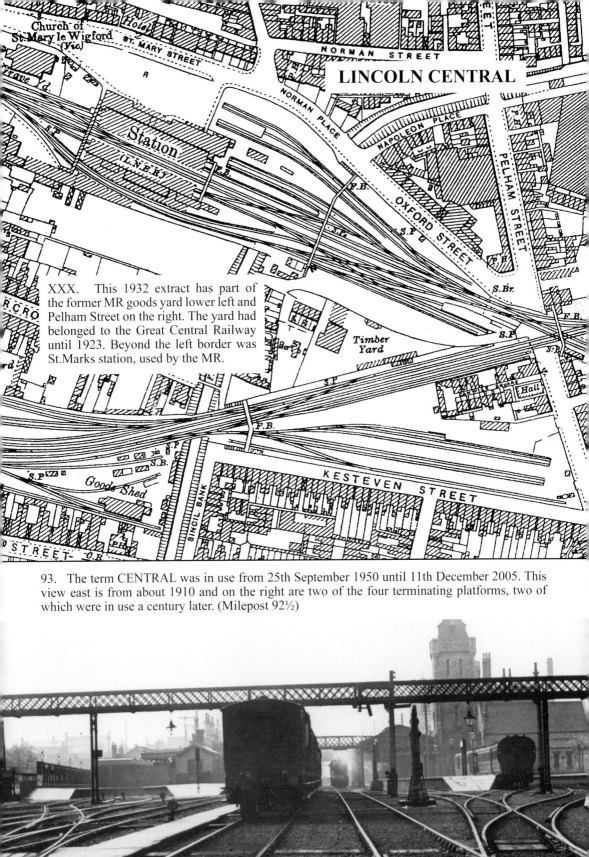

LINCOLN CENTRAL

XXX. This 1932 extract has part of the former MR goods yard lower left and Pelham Street on the right. The yard had belonged to the Great Central Railway until 1923. Beyond the left border was St.Marks station, used by the MR.

93. The term CENTRAL was in use from 25th September 1950 until 11th December 2005. This view east is from about 1910 and on the right are two of the four terminating platforms, two of which were in use a century later. (Milepost 92½)

94.   Class B1 4-6-0 no. 1269 is working the 3.30pm March to Doncaster service on 9th May 1949 and still carries LNER on its tender. The long footbridge carried pedestrians, not passengers; see map. (W.A.Camwell/SLS)

95.   Approaching the station backwards in about 1953 is an ex-GCR 4-6-2T. A Ford truck waits inside the gates on the often congested crossing. Half its name is evident on the right. (P.Ward/SLS)

96. Class C4 4-4-2 no. 2918 is arriving on 11th September 1948 with a train composed of six coaches from Lowestoft and five from Yarmouth, all bound for York. The rear ones are on Durham Ox Crossing. It was named after the white inn on the left. The bold advertisement states "Lincoln the home of Ruston Oil Engines", now known as diesels. The firm also produced a wide range of civil engineering equipment. (V.R.Webster/SLS)

> **Other views can be seen in the** *Boston to Lincoln,*
> *Lincoln to Cleethorpes* **and** *Nottingham to Lincoln* **albums**
> **from Middleton Press.**

6640	2nd-SINGLE / SINGLE-2nd	6640
	BLANKNEY & **METHERINGHAM TO**	
	Blankney & M. Blankney & M. LINCOLN (Central) LINCOLN (Central)	
	LINCOLN (CENTRAL)	
	(E) 2/2 Fare 2/2 (E) For conditions see over For conditions see over	

0843	**2nd - DAY RETURN** Re-opening of Metheringham Station To be available any train any date Monday, 6th October to Saturday, 18th October Excluding Sunday, 12th October	0843
	Metheringham to	
	LINCOLN (CENTRAL) AND BACK	
	(E) (E) For conditions see over For conditions see over	

97.   The terminal platforms and the public footbridge are largely obscured by the steam from class J69 0-6-0T no. 68599 on 14th July 1959. (Bentley coll.)

98.   The 12.54pm Doncaster to March is headed by class V2 2-6-2 no. 60870 on 18th February 1961. It is taking water, while a DMU runs into platform 7. Three coaches are berthed on the right. Beyond the footbridge is the outline of the new Pelham Street Bridge. (J.Langford)

99. Seen on 9th May 1964 are parcels in profusion, the bridge for passengers, an old signal post carrying modern colour lights and pilot engine no. D2277, resting in the distance. (J.Langford)

100. This bridge was built in 1958-59 to eliminate the Durham Ox crossing, but the inn had to be demolished to make space for it. No. 31173 is passing on 28th July 1979 with the 09.19 Manchester to Yarmouth service, while the splendid cathedral graces the scene, on high ground. (T.Heavyside)

101.   Seen on the same day is no. 37110, which is departing with the 08.35 Newcastle to Yarmouth. Track reduction had taken place; the two on the right went later. (T.Heavyside)

LINCOLN

102.   Star of the show on 21st June 2008 was class A4 4-6-2 no. 60007 *Sir Nigel Gresley*. "The Cathedrals Express" was operated by Steam Dreams and was running back to King's Cross, at 16.40. It had left there at 09.18, behind class mate no. 60019 *Bittern*. (J.Whitehouse)

103.   East Midland Trains' no. 153376 reaches journey's end at 10.59 in bay platform 2 with the 09.35 ex-Peterborough. No. 153376 was named *X24-Expeditious* at Lincoln on 10th April 2014 to commemorate the 70th anniversary of the launch of the World War II midget submarine of the same name, the sole survivor of its type. The DMU was built by Marshalls of Gainsborough. We finish our visit to Lincoln with four views from 17th July 2014. (A.C.Hartless)

104.   EMT's no. 153310 has arrived at Platform 4 with the 10.50 from Newark Northgate. On the left is Platform 3, with its Baronial tower. To its right is a sympathetically designed lift tower giving step-free access to the footbridge linking the two sides of the station, across four running lines. Beyond that are bay platforms 1 and 2; when the station was at its largest there were two further bays to their left. In the background, no. 153376 is passing under Pelham Street Bridge as it leaves forming the 11.10 to Peterborough. (A.C.Hartless)

105. The view west is from the station footbridge. On the left, no. 153310 stands at Platform 4 with the 11.35 to Newark Northgate. At Platform 3, no. 153374 is arriving with the 10.24 from Doncaster. Pedestrians stream across High Street level crossing in the background following the latter's passage. Note also the signal gantry spanning the tracks at the platform ends. Also evident is High Street box, which earlier had a 36-lever frame working. It closed on 19th July 2008. (A.C.Hartless)

106.   The prospective passenger's perspective. Lincoln station in 2014 was well cared for, and a splendid survivor of Victorian Tudor, built in 1848. The symmetry and detailing is magnificent, spoilt only by a tree. (A.C.Hartless)

2. Navenby Route

Bracebridge Gas Sidings

XXXI.   The location can be seen near the lower border of map XXIII, near picture 89. This 1907 extract reveals the extent of the private sidings. The works started in 1876 and the tonnage of coal consumed annually was about 150,000 tons, at its maximum. The connection from Lincoln was retained until 6th November 1970, when the 32-lever signal box was shut. The route south to Honington closed in 1965. There had been three extra sidings known as "The Field" east of the running lines, but dates are not known. Similarly, there were more further south on the east side, for Bracebridge Brickworks. Here, there was a 20-lever signal box from 1877 to 1st November 1965.

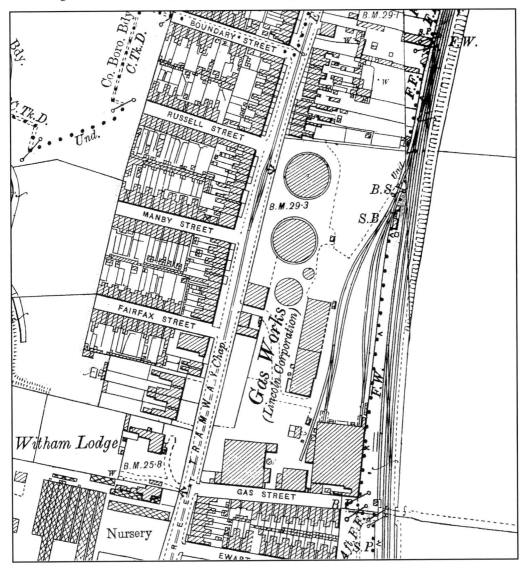

WADDINGTON

XXXII. The 1901 revision was produced when the population was 770. The station was about one mile west of the village. A massive RAF camp was created to the east of it, on ground once used for horse racing. The village was subjected to severe bombing and loss of life in World War II. It had 6086 residents in 2001; the RAF was still busy nearby.

L. N. E. R.
FOR CONDITIONS SEE BACK. Available for
three days, including day of issue.
NAVENBY TO
KING'S CROSS
Fare / S / 18s. 8d C
THIRD / 138 / CLASS.
King's Cross
7920   7920

107. The local quarry produced limestone, but the main traffic was agricultural. This was the view south in about 1939 and includes the 25-lever signal box, which was in use until goods cessation on 1st November 1965. Passenger traffic ended on 10th September 1962. (Stations UK)

HARMSTON

XXXIII. The village was to the east of the line and housed 327 in 1901. The map is from 1905. The signal box is by the level crossing, on the left. It closed on 1st November 1965, with the line.

108. Looking south in 1955, we see spacious accommodation for the station master, mostly on the upper floor. In 1922, there were six stopping trains each way on the route, weekdays only. (Stations UK)

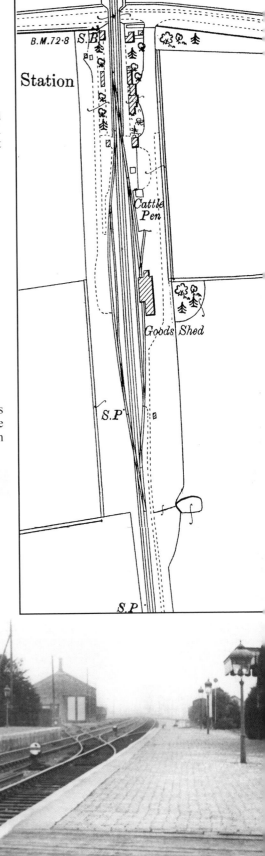

109.   All traffic ceased on 10th September 1962. The photograph is from October 1967. The tall chimney pot is above the station laundry area, above the clothes boiler. Staff dwellings are on the left. (J.A.Evans)

NAVENBY

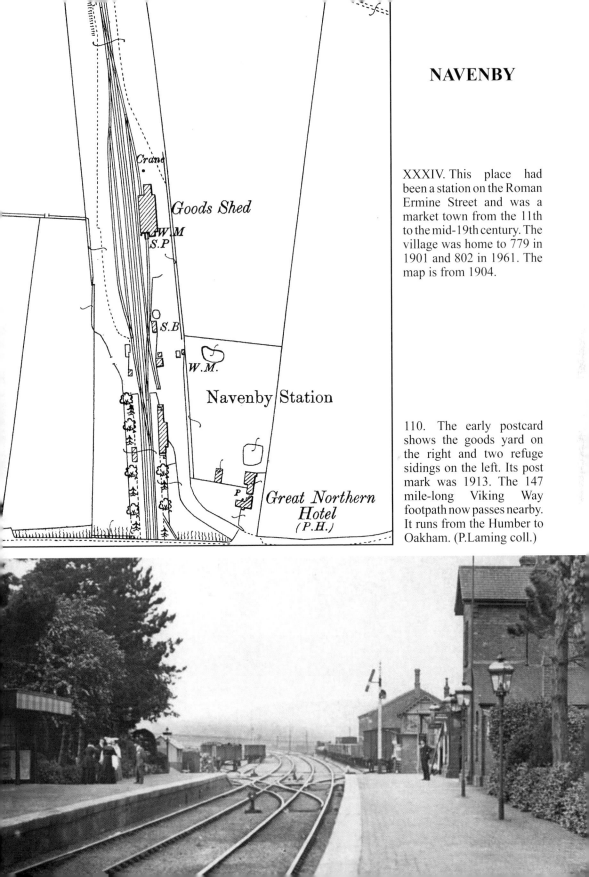

XXXIV. This place had been a station on the Roman Ermine Street and was a market town from the 11th to the mid-19th century. The village was home to 779 in 1901 and 802 in 1961. The map is from 1904.

Crane

Goods Shed

W.M
S.P

S.B

W.M.

Navenby Station

P

Great Northern Hotel (P.H.)

110. The early postcard shows the goods yard on the right and two refuge sidings on the left. Its post mark was 1913. The 147 mile-long Viking Way footpath now passes nearby. It runs from the Humber to Oakham. (P.Laming coll.)

111.   It is 26th June 1933 and class D2 no. 4377 is working the 6.20pm Lincoln to Grantham mixed train. Passenger service ceased here on 10th September 1962. (H.C.Casserley)

112. This view is in the other direction on the same day and includes the passenger crossing, which has a rodding tunnel for the remote points. Cheap brick was used here; local stone had been demanded for some other stations on the route. (H.C.Casserley)

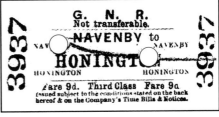

3937   G.   N.   R.
Not transferable.
NAVENBY to
NAV   NAVENBY
HONINGT
HONINGTON   HONINGTON
fare 9d. Third Class Fare 9d.
Issued subject to the conditions stated on the back
hereof & on the Company's Time Bills & Notices.
3937

2409   2nd-FORCES LEAVE   FORCES LEAVE-2nd   2409
SINGLE   SINGLE
Leadenham to
Leadenham   Leadenham
Grantham, etc.   Grantham, etc.
GRANTHAM or LINCOLN (CENTRAL)
(E)   2/4   Fare   2/4   (E)
For conditions see over   For conditions see over

113.   A panorama from the road bridge completes our survey. The goods shed hides the crane, which had a rating of 4 tons 18cwt. The yard closed on 15th June 1964. The station gardens competition award was keenly sought. (Stations UK)

LEADENHAM

XXXV. The 1949 issue at 6ins to 1 mile includes a long loop with a siding on the west side. The yard had a 6-ton crane listed in 1938, and there was a private siding to the north for the Barnstone Cement Company. A 2ft 6ins gauge railway with a cable incline had run northeast from the yard to fetch ironstone in about 1890 to 1920.

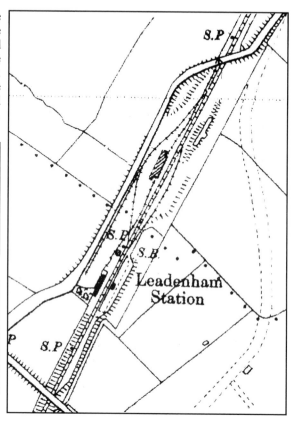

0567 0567

3rd-SINGLE FORCES LEAVE

CAYTHORPE to

KING'S CROSS LONDON

(E)   Fare 12/1 H

FOR CONDITIONS SEE OVER

0003 0003

L. N. E. R.
EXCHANGE TICKET
FOR CONDITIONS SEE BACK

CAYTHORPE to

LINCOLN

Available only on date shewn hereon.
Not available intermediately or for break of
Journey. Issued in exchange for return half of
Lincolnshire Road Car Co. Ltd. ticket

THIRD CLASS SUPPLEMENT 2s.2d.

114. The Royal Train was frequently berthed overnight in the long siding from the mid-1940s to the mid-1960s; night time was peaceful here. The 30-lever signal box closed with the line in November 1965. (LOSA)

June 1964 timetable.

Week Days

Miles			am	Commences 30th September	am	Not after 28th September	am		am		am	Except Saturdays	am		pm		pm	(Via Sleaford)	pm		pm
2	London (King's C) dep	4 0		8A 0		8B 0	..	8 20	..	10 20	..		11P20	..	1 0	..	2 20	..	..	4 20
—	Grantham dep	8 0		9 43		9 52	....	10 33	....	12 18 pm	....		1 20	....	2 54	....	4 22	....	5 13	....	6 23
12¼	Leadenham	8 18		10 1		10 10	..	10 51	..	12 36	....			..	3 12	..	4 40		..		6 41
24¼	Lincoln (Central) arr	8 35		10 18		10 27	....	11 8	....	12 53	....		1 54	....	3 29	....	4 57	....	6 14	....	6 58

Week Days—continued | | | | | | Sundays

		pm		pm		pm						am		pm		pm			
2	London (King's C) dep	5 5	..	6 40	..	8 20	..	..	..	..	..	1020	..	3C 0	..	5 45	..	..	..
	Grantham dep	7 17	....	8 40	....	1027	....				..	1 5 pm	....	5 24	....	8 0	....		
	Leadenham	7 35	..	8 58	..	1045	..	..	..	..	..	1 23	..	5 42	..	8 18	..	..	..
	Lincoln (Central) arr	7 52	....	9 15	....	11 2	....				..	1 40	....	5 59	....	8 35	....		

Week Days

Miles			am		am	Via Sleaford	am			am		am		pm		pm		Saturdays only	pm
—	Lincoln (Central) dep	6 40	....	7 15		7 30	....		8 56	....	10 15	....	1230	....	2 0	....		3 39
12¼	Leadenham dep	6 56	..	7 31	..				9 12	..	10 31	..	1246	..	2 16	..		3 55
24¼	Grantham arr	7 17	....	7 52	..	9 1	....		9 33	....	10 52	....	1 7	....	2 37	....		4 16
130	2 London (King's C) arr	9 40	..	9 50	..		..	..	11 38	..	1 9	..	3 11	..	4 51	..		..

Week Days—continued | | | | | | Sundays

		Except Saturdays	pm	Saturdays only	pm	Except Saturdays	pm	Via Sleaford	pm	pm	Via Sleaford	pm	pm				pm		pm		pm
	Lincoln (Central) dep		3 43		4 40		4 46		4 58	6 35		7 35	8 37	....	....	....	12 5	....	4 15	....	6 50
	Leadenham		3 59		4 56	..	5 2			6 51	..		8 53	..	..	..	1221	..	4 31	..	7 6
	Grantham arr		4 20		5 17	....	5 23		6 20	7 12	....	8 33	9 14	....	....	....	1242	....	4 52	....	7 27
	2 London (King's C) arr		6615		7 23	..		7 33		8 19	9 18	..	..	2D56 am	..	..	..	3 24	..	7 18	..	9 44

A Dep King's Cross 5 55 am on Saturdays and on 24th, 25th, 26th December, 1st January, 26th, 27th, 30th March, 15th and 18th May

B On Saturdays dep King's Cross 5 55 am

C Until 27th October dep King's Cross 3 10 pm

D On Sunday mornings arr King's Cross 3 31 am

G Does not apply on 24th, 25th, 26th December, 26th, 27th, 30th March, 15th and 18th May. Pullman Cars only Grantham to King's Cross. Supplementary charges

P Does not apply on 24th, 25th, 26th December, 26th, 27th, 30th March, 15th and 18th May. Pullman Cars only King's Cross to Grantham. Supplementary charges

115.   The entrance was on the west side and could be used by passengers more than three years longer than all the other stations on the route. Closure came on 1st November 1965. The goods yard closed on 15th June 1964. The west facade is seen in 1982, when the building had become a private house. (HMRS)

CAYTHORPE

116. The chairman of the GNR lived nearby and he had his own personal waiting room here. Up to 1914, there were two Lincoln expresses, which he could stop. Local iron working ceased in 1930, mainly. (P.Laming coll.)

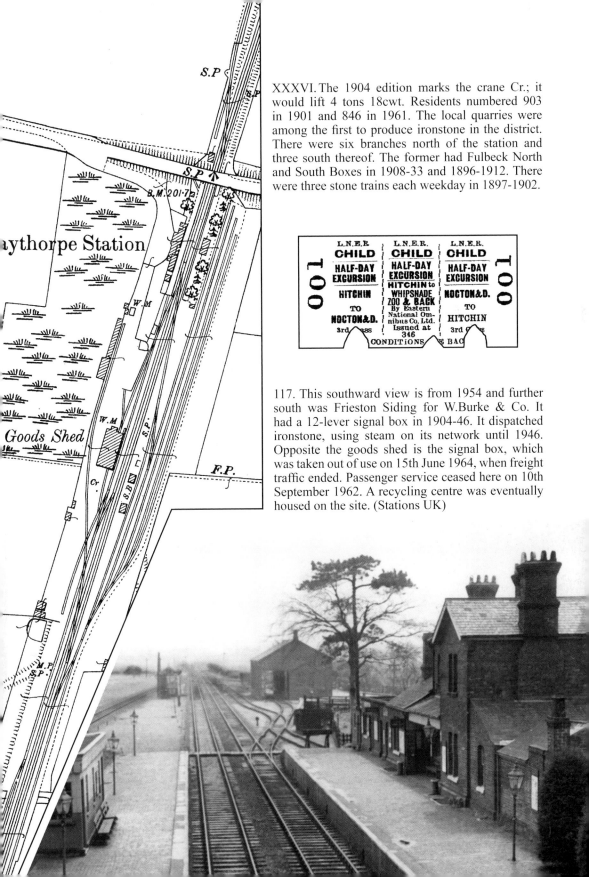

S.P

S.P

S.P

B.M.201·7a

W.M

aythorpe Station

W.M

Goods Shed

S.B

Cr.

F.P.

M.P.
S.P.

XXXVI. The 1904 edition marks the crane Cr.; it would lift 4 tons 18cwt. Residents numbered 903 in 1901 and 846 in 1961. The local quarries were among the first to produce ironstone in the district. There were six branches north of the station and three south thereof. The former had Fulbeck North and South Boxes in 1908-33 and 1896-1912. There were three stone trains each weekday in 1897-1902.

L.N.E.R. CHILD HALF-DAY EXCURSION HITCHIN TO NOCTON&D. 3rd ess	L.N.E.R. CHILD HALF-DAY EXCURSION HITCHIN to WHIPSNADE ZOO & BACK By Eastern National Omnibus Co. Ltd. Issued at 346 CONDITIONS	L.N.E.R. CHILD HALF-DAY EXCURSION NOCTON&D. TO HITCHIN 3rd BAC

100 ... **100**

117. This southward view is from 1954 and further south was Frieston Siding for W.Burke & Co. It had a 12-lever signal box in 1904-46. It dispatched ironstone, using steam on its network until 1946. Opposite the goods shed is the signal box, which was taken out of use on 15th June 1964, when freight traffic ended. Passenger service ceased here on 10th September 1962. A recycling centre was eventually housed on the site. (Stations UK)

HONINGTON

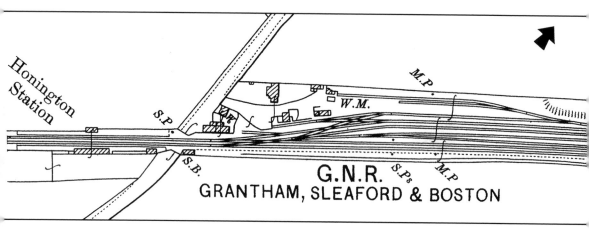

XXXVII. The 1903 edition has the Boston to Nottingham line from right to left and the Lincoln line diverging from it. There were only 189 residents in 1901.

For other views, see our *Nottingham to Boston*
album, pictures 75-77.

118. This view is from the level crossing in the 1930s and includes a long refuge siding beyond the right platform. Passengers changing here had to use the road crossing. (Stations UK)

119. Running in from Boston some time in 1956 is class A5 4-6-2T no. 69827, ex-LNER. Curving left is the Lincoln route. Passenger service ceased here on 10th September 1962. (C.L.Caddy coll.)

120. The signal box has the suffix JUNCTION, but the station did not. The goods yard was in use until 27th April 1964. A view from about 1970 shows only one signal arm left and a coal stove still usable in the box, which closed on 29th July 1984. At least, trains still speed through here. (LOSA)

MP Middleton Press

EVOLVING THE ULTIMATE RAIL ENCYCLOPEDIA

Easebourne Midhurst GU29 9AZ. Tel:01730 813169

www.middletonpress.co.uk · email:info@middletonpress.co.uk

A-978 0 906520   B- 978 1 873793   C- 978 1 901706   D-978 1 904474
E -978 1 906008   F - 978 1 908174